Grace Space

Creating Spaces We Want to Live and Lead In

Other Books by Heather Penny

The Life You're Made For

The Life You're Made For, Coaching Companion

The Bracelet

Grace Space

Creating Spaces We Want to Live and Lead In

3C Living and Leading Series

HEATHER PENNY, PhD

Copyright © 2024 by Heather Penny

Edited by Natalie Hanemann, Hanemann Editorial

Cover design by Kristen Ingebretson

Interior formatting by Lorie DeWorken, Mind the Margins

All rights reserved. No part of this publication may be reproduced, stored in a retrieval system, or transmitted in any form or by any means—electronic, mechanical, photocopy, recording, or any other—without prior written permission from the author.

ISBN: 979-8-218-17420-0 (print)

To my favorite son, Luke Maximus,
who committed to helping his mom create spaces of
grace when she had never raised a teenage son before.

Contents

Foreword xv

3C Living and Leading Series xix

Introduction: Who I Am and What I Do. 1

1. Responding vs. Reacting 11

2. Questioning vs. Accusing 25

3. Receptivity vs. Defensiveness 35

4. Constructive vs. Destructive Communication. . . 45

5. Connection vs. Protection 55

6. Freedom vs. Control. 75

7. Trust vs. Fear 87

The Wrap-Up. 101

Bibliography 105

Acknowledgments. 107

About Dr. Heather Penny 109

Foreword

Does the world really need one more leadership book?

That was my first thought when Heather told me about the book she was working on. Yawn.

But when she started to unpack the premise for *Grace Space*, I found myself actually getting excited. Like "write this book already" kind of excited. And now that I've read it, the answer is yes. Yes, the world needs this leadership book.

For almost 20 years I've watched Heather watch leaders. She studies them. In corporate and not-for-profit settings, in politics, elite athletics, churches, and in education. Heather has coached, challenged, and cared for some of the best leaders around the globe. She's also listened and learned. What do these great leaders have in common? Is there some sort of "secret sauce"?

Again, yes. The recipe is the book you hold in your hand. Grace space is that intersection of hard truth and human kindness, of reality and humanity, of performance and personhood. It's not just a corporate concept. I didn't have the language for it (until now) but in my work over the years as director of two national not-for-profits, and now on a more organic level as a relationship coach, it's exactly what I help couples and parents and siblings and colleagues and friends do: create spaces of grace. Spaces where we confront our inherent selfishness and begin to heal our brokenness. Where we are heard and valued. Where we can "speak the truth in love."

Writer Timothy Keller said it this way: "Love without truth is sentimentality; it supports and affirms us but keeps us in denial about our flaws. Truth without love is harshness; it gives us information but in such a way that we cannot really hear it."

Heather offers seven new ways of thinking about our relationships—work relationships for sure, but all relationships. To approach people with truth in ways they can hear it. Seven ways to think differently, each with practical, actionable steps to reprogram the way we lead. Because good leaders don't just lead, they lead people.

That's not just a well-worn phrase for Heather. She not only writes and coaches these principles, she lives them. To be with her is to enter a beautiful space of grace.

If you take this book to heart, it will change your leadership. But it could also change your life.

Sharol Josephson
National Director, FamilyLife Canada
former Canadian Director, Operation Christmas Child

Advanced Acclaim

"I want to live in the Grace Space that Heather leads us to discover. This space is for us all. It is *not* too good to be true, but a reality that we can all give and receive. Read it with an open heart and mind, and you will be changed. I know I was."
— Bob Goff, Author of *New York Times* Bestsellers: *Love Does*, *Everybody Always*, *Dream Big*, and *Undistracted*

"What quality differentiates the people who serve others from the ones who serve only themselves? It's *grace*. In author Heather Penny's words, grace is 'a welcoming space that starts from within and invites others to join us in the space between.' I hope you read *Grace Space* and learn from Heather about the freedom that comes when you extend grace to others at home, at work, and in your community."
— Ken Blanchard, Coauthor of *The New One Minute Manager®* and *Simple Truths of Leadership*

"One of this book's strengths lies in its ability to bridge the gap between theory and practical application. Dr. Penny provides actionable insights that readers can readily implement in their leadership roles, fostering a workplace culture that not only values performance but also prioritizes the well-being and growth of its members. By emphasizing the importance of emotional intelligence, communication, and fostering a sense of purpose, *Grace Space* empowers leaders to create environments where both individuals and the collective thrive."
— Christopher Panagiotu, CFP®, CRPS®, The "CAP" in CAPitalize, Wealth Manager, CAPitalize Your Finances, LLC

"*Grace Space* feels like a breath of fresh air, a voice that comes alongside you and gently offers you the encouragement you need to grow into the best version of yourself, and to help the people you lead to do the same. But this book isn't all hypotheticals and big ideas, it also offers practical wisdom and takeaways that you can start applying immediately."
— Sharon McMahon, Creator of Sharon Says So

"Heather has a way of communicating that reaches everyone from creatives to the business community to athletes to pastors and to everyone in between. *Grace Space* is the handbook to leadership and needs to be on everyone's bookshelf."
— Jason Squires, Creative Coach and Director of *The Creative Launch*

"Powerfully practical, *Grace Space* should be required reading for anyone in leadership (or for anyone who works with people in any capacity!). With no fluff and so many actionable learnings, this was a refreshing and truly useful read."
— Kate Shepherd, Founder, Morning Moon Studios, and Host of Top 1% Podcast "The Creative Genius"

"Life is not a talent contest, it's a strategy game. Few works offer practical, executable guidance to turn theories into reality, but Dr. Penny tackles the deepest human values—courage, trust, and dignity—by digging into the relatable 'spaces' between the ideas. *Grace Space* delivers an understanding of our collective humanity that shows us how to treat others with empathy and compassion to transform the soul."
— Tom Murphy, Sweethearts & Heroes

"In *Grace Space*, Dr. Heather Penny brilliantly underscores the invaluable currency of connection in today's fragmented world. While numerous books touch upon leadership qualities, this work delves deep into the heart of relational leadership, proving that genuine connections form the bedrock of influential leadership and collective progress. The book elevates the notion of 'grace spaces' from a conceptual realm to practical, actionable steps. Readers are not only shown the transformative power of connecting and building bridges but are also handed the tools to create and join these spaces, allowing the cultivation of enriched environments wherever they go. *Grace Space* is a clarion call for leaders and individuals alike to embrace connection over protection and collaboration over isolation, championing a message of unity, optimism, and collective heroism."
— Jennifer Morton, Chief Executive Officer, Association of Golf Merchandisers (AGM)

"Not only is this a phenomenal book for executives and entrepreneurs alike, but a handy blueprint for business aspirants. Readers will gain the tools to not only enhance their professional goals but their personal lives as well. *Grace Space* proves to be a keystone in the work/life balance."
— Ash Brown, CEO of Ash Said It LLC

"Leadership matters, and it is hard. Heather Penny provides seven practices for how to lead and live in 'grace space.' With her practical ideas, warmth, and vulnerability everyone will find something in this book to be a better leader and person."
— Jodi Davis, Leadership Coach, Retired Philanthropy Executive

"We all can choose to foster grace in our workplace, home, and community. Heather Penny has given us seven concrete and doable practices to make grace a reality so our world functions better and is a kinder place."
— Paula Allison, Chief Advancement Officer, Los Rios Community College District

"In a world where it feels like we're repeatedly told to be the best and beat the rest, we need Dr. Heather Penny's voice in our ear. *Grace Space* isn't just a great read, it's a rally cry to create places where people really see and appreciate each other. Leading with grace isn't just the right thing to do; it's smart and sustainable for building strong, successful organizations and communities."
— Ken Morton, Jr., VP Retail & Marketing, Morton Golf, LLC
  - Haggin Oaks GC – Bing Maloney GC – Bartley Cavanaugh GC – William Land GC

"Dr. Penny redefines the intersection of leadership and humanity with compelling practicality and profound insight. *Grace Space* provides a powerful blueprint for how anyone can lead through compassion and trust to create safer, more productive communities and workplaces through the power of grace."
— Dr. John Harris, Executive Coach

"*Grace Space* is everything I've come to expect in a Heather Penny book—up-to-date research, inspiring examples, numbered steps, practical tips, and engaging writing. As the first book in Heather's 3C Living and Leading series, *Grace Space* aims to help readers move beyond 'safe spaces' to create both an authentic 'space within' for the self as well as welcoming and inclusive 'spaces between' for others. Readers will feel like they are receiving personal coaching from Heather as they encounter specific conversation starters and responses, role plays, best practices, and applicable illustrations from Heather's vast coaching experience in both corporate and individual settings. *Grace Space* is a valuable and unique handbook for leaders who want to imaginatively and effectively create space for those they lead and support to flourish and achieve."
— Lisa Smith, PhD, Author of *Hammer & Fire: Lessons on Spiritual Passion from the Writings and Life of George Whitefield*, English professor, Pepperdine University

"*Grace Space* is a must-read that helps us incorporate the transformative power of grace in our lives, both personally and professionally. In a world where thoughtfulness, honor, courtesy, and fairness may seem elusive, this book reminds us of their importance and equips us with concrete practices to infuse grace into our daily interactions. Grace has the power to make us better leaders, parents, spouses, and friends. Heather Penny's *Grace Space* gives us practical strategies for increasing grace in our lives."
— Stephanie Nelson, Author of *Imagine More: Do What You Love, Discover Your Potential*

"This book provides a valuable opportunity for leaders to pause amid a fast-paced world and engage in essential introspection, ultimately yielding positive outcomes for themselves and those they lead. It skillfully highlights the subtle nuances within each of us, encouraging a deeper exploration for boundless personal and professional growth."
— Rev. Christian B. Aaron, RN, MDiv.

"*Grace Space* is more than a mere book; it's a transformative movement urging a vital shift in the business culture we urgently need. In an age where grace has been scarce, now is the moment to weave it into the very fabric of our business landscape. Beyond catalyzing a necessary cultural transformation, *Grace Space* draws us to embrace what's naturally within us—grace and kindness. This isn't just a read; it's a call to live and lead in a way that resonates with the core of who we are as individuals and as a community. To lead this way is beautiful."
— Erica Dvorak, Founder and Creative Director of Faith & Gather, Host of the Faith Inspired Podcast

"Heather Penny's latest book, *Grace Space*, is a powerful, relatable, and actionable narrative that is both personal and practical. It is a must-read for anyone who wants to bring grace beyond the concept of 'safe spaces' and become more proactive in creating it in our workplaces and communities. The book is concise and relatable, with Heather presenting seven practice areas that are backed up by rationale, examples, and tips that can help us improve our abilities and create a 'grace space' for ourselves and those around us."
— Sarah Boxx, CEO and Chief Vision Sherpa at Sarah Boxx LLC

"The demands on leaders today require a new way of framing our interactions, our management, and our purpose. Heather's timely insights offer a literal 'grace space' to consider practical approaches to our roles and our impact that may very well change our workplaces and lives for years to come."
— Laura Cootsona, Founder, Good | Well Consulting

"In *Grace Space*, Heather Penny serves as a breath of fresh air! Her wisdom and real-world approach to becoming a high-impact leader give readers the tools they need to successfully navigate today's complex environment with dignity and emotional intelligence. If you want to upgrade your servant leadership skills with battle-tested strategies you can use right now, read this book!"
— Tammy Alvarez, CEO, Career Winners Circle, and Author of *Escaping the Career Trap: Transform Your Apathy into Ambition and Never Hate Mondays Again*

"A Must-Read... Dr. Heather Penny underscores relational attributes so desperately sought today: tools for strengthening emotional intelligence, guides to foster courageous curiosity, permission to be vulnerable and seek support, creating connections through compassion while embracing transparency, and growing trust. As someone who has served in ministry and led national and global teams, I implore you to read and ponder the principles of *Grace Space* in order to invest in your own personal growth as well as become more passionate in leading others well."
— Julie Roe, PhD, Retired Nonprofit Executive and Adjunct Professor

"The challenges of being a leader in such a rapidly changing world require leaders to find unchanging truths and principles like the ones found on the pages of *Grace Space*. Few authors have more clearly articulated how to create and maintain a grace-based culture that will stand the test of time. Heather's tried and true principles of grace will truly help relieve the stress of trying to create a 'new and improved edition' of your leadership team. You just have to make space for grace."
— Don DeLair, Founding Headmaster, King's Schools

"*Grace Space* is an important addition to the business book market. It makes the important point that leadership is a skill that begins inside us. The book emphasizes that good leaders need the ability to see things clearly, to have confidence in their vision, and the courage to implement it. In order to be effective, leaders need the skills to respond positively to conflict, know how to be fair, and to provide a safe space where people can reach their full potential. This wonderful book is a must for anyone who is a supervisor, manager, or CEO in any industry. I wish it had been available when I was in business. It's full of useful ideas and the information is presented in a warm, conversational tone and is easy to absorb. And lucky us: *Grace Space* is the first book in a series of three. I highly recommend it."
— Susan Salenger, Author of *Sidelined: How Women Can Navigate a Broken Healthcare System*

3C Living and Leading Series

I've created the 3C Living and Leading series as a way to help leaders grow their soft skills—in business, at home, and in the world. I knew *Grace Space* had to be the inaugural book in the series because it establishes the foundation of good leadership. Good leaders learn skills to improve the way they interact with their team members, and this helps improve productivity.

We grow Grace Spaces when we lead with the 3Cs: Clarity, Confidence, and Courage. Clarity is about seeing what is true, confidence is about aligning with beliefs that inspire, and courage is about taking the steps that move us forward. Leading with these 3Cs consistently helps us to instill trust in our people and in ourselves.

No one is born a great leader. It takes time and experience and hard work. These lessons can be expedited when we are mentored, but even then, a leader becomes great when they are put in hundreds of challenging situations and are forced to figure out the best course of action, not only for their team and the company as a whole but for the environments they influence.

The world is hungry for more leaders who will do the right thing, model a positive response to conflict, and choose the path of fairness and accountability. If it were easy, we would be bursting at the seams with excellent leaders. Part of understanding the 3C model is realizing that we require time to ourselves to gain clarity on how we're feeling and what we want. We learn ways to grow our confidence so we won't listen to the mind chatter that whispers false beliefs to us. We exercise our courage muscle so it becomes easier to use. Great leadership starts from within and it takes a great leader attending to the whole person—body, mind, heart, and spirit.

My hope is that this series of books will help you learn how to go after the life you were uniquely made to live, because you are exactly what the world needs.

Let's get started!

> Out beyond ideas of wrongdoing and rightdoing, there is a field. I'll meet you there. When the soul lies down in that grass, the world is too full to talk about. Ideas, language, even the phrase "each other" doesn't make any sense.
>
> *–Rumi*

Introduction:
Who I Am and What I Do

Contributing to the well-being of others and empowering them to reach their unique potential has motivated me for the past several decades. This focus has become the heartbeat for the work I do, the life I lead, and the person I am daily choosing to become. As a leadership coach working with individuals and teams, I have looked for ways to foster trust, open lines of communication, and build bridges between people and the unique perspectives they each hold.

My love for learning and my curious nature have made me an observer of life, of people, and of behaviors. In all fairness, with there being nothing new under the sun, these observations build on the theories and ideas of the innovative souls who have gone before me. After years of reading and listening to these brilliant thinkers, I noticed something . . . a thread woven into the text and subtext of all these great ideas. It is the idea of spaces. Where we show up and how we engage—with ourselves and with one another.

Parker Palmer, American author and activist in education and spirituality, writes about the necessity of creating "spaces within and spaces between us that welcome the wisdom of the soul."[1] This has been a phrase that I have noodled on for years as I hold the synergistic value for being mindful of who I am choosing to become, along with how I am impacting the spaces I step into. Who we are internally influences what we bring to our external world.

Respected leaders know that inspiring leadership starts from within. The values we hold, the perspectives we develop, and the character we cultivate all make up who we are and who we are choosing to become. Our space within. Only then has a person earned the right to lead others in the spaces between. How we welcome others into our spaces is the difference maker. Do we want to be known as a welcoming leader or a closed leader? Welcoming leaders inspire change. Closed leaders own the space and make us stand outside of it while they dictate their orders.

Several great thought leaders have gone before us in creating welcoming spaces. Madeleine L'Engle, author of *A Wrinkle in Time*, was known for her ability to create

---

[1] Parker Palmer, ***A Hidden Wholeness*** (San Francisco, Jossey-Bass, 2009), 49.

characters who broke cultural boundaries and celebrated the unusual. In her day, young women were rarely protagonists and grown women didn't write science fiction. L'Engle's quirky, outcast characters reflected her own struggles growing up. She created a space in children's worlds to be odd and okay, normalizing offbeat behavior.

> When Madeleine was 12, her parents moved to Europe and abruptly deposited her at the Chatelard School in Switzerland, an elite all-girls boarding school where she felt abandoned, alienated, and shattered by the loss of privacy. Surrounded by cliquish and petty peers, under the watchful eyes of school matrons, Madeleine was forced to develop a new skill: an impenetrable "force field of silence" that she could inhabit like a magical cloak. "Within that force field, I could go on writing my stories and my poems and dreaming my dreams," she said in an interview decades later. It was an effective tool, and one that would always serve her creatively.[2]

History tells the story of a space that, for a short time, ended all adversity so a meaningful connection could be made. On Christmas Day in 1914, soldiers fighting on both sides along the Western Front during World War I created a welcoming space of peace. German soldiers began lighting candles on small Christmas trees in the days leading up to Christmas. The British and French responded by serenading the opposing forces with songs and tossing gifts over enemy lines. They each

---

[2] "Madeleine L'Engle Biographical Sketch / Page 3 of 4." https://www.madeleinelengle.com/madeleine-lengle/madeleine-lengle-biography-3/

emerged under a banner of truth to bury their dead, break bread together, and even exchange gifts. The ripple effect was so profound that when the superiors ordered them to commence fighting the following day, each side purposely aimed high to miss hitting one another. The officers on both sides had to bring in new troops to finish the battle.[3]

Viktor Frankl, a prisoner who survived two concentration camps, created a welcoming space in his mind that had a rippling effect. While he endured inhumane conditions and lost all his family members, he didn't respond with depression and vitriol. "The last of human freedoms," Frankl wrote, is "to choose one's attitude, in any given set of circumstances."[4] He chose to respond by thinking of the love he had for his wife. He also saw the value of retaining a sense of humor during the violent horrors he endured. He encouraged his fellow prisoners to hold on to hope in some of the darkest moments in human history. He chose to carry his space "with him" as he held on to the only freedom he had. His most well-known quote, and one of the key components of my idea of Grace Space, states, "Between stimulus and response there is a space. In that space is our power to choose our response. In our response lies our growth and our freedom."[5]

The ability to choose how we respond is what makes us different from the animals. We have a nanosecond to decide if we're going to return evil for evil . . . if we're going to return

---

[3] Stanley Weintraub, ***Silent Night*** (New York City, Plume, 2002).
[4] Viktor Frankl, ***Man's Search for Meaning*** (Boston, Beacon Press, reprint 2006).
[5] Frankl, ***Man's Search***.

love for hate. Many of us don't exercise our free will well; when pushed, we choose to push back harder. We give up the very dignity of our humanity and can often allow ourselves to be reactive and victimized by the meanest person in the room. In doing this, we lose our sense of self because we stop exercising a nobility of choice that says, *I don't have to react in this moment to their violence, anger, and hatred. I can respond with love and goodness and kindness.*

Great thought leaders like L'Engle and Frankl are inspiring to read about, but how do we take the wisdom of those who have gone before us and apply it to the modern workplace? After all, it is inevitable that uncomfortable situations will arise—personalities clash, intense business situations create impatience, and tempers flare. We aren't always careful with the words or tone we use. "The most common leadership failures don't involve fraud, the embezzlement of funds, or sex scandals. It is more common to see leaders fail in the area of every day self-management."[6]

This book will be a guide as we examine sticky situations leaders face and learn how to use tools that aid in avoiding leadership failures and growing from failures we were unable to avoid. It also serves to develop our presence and the space we choose to offer—whether in the workplace, our homes, or in day-to-day interactions in the world we live in. Creating spaces of grace is about being a better human and inspiring others to join us.

---

[6] Lou Solomon, *Empathy, Chapter 6* (Boston, MA: Harvard Business Review Press, 2017), 64.

It isn't only past figures who have helped us make great strides in improving the business environment. Some of today's leading voices are starting imperative conversations that further the conversation on the topic of leadership growth. Thanks to the research of leaders such as Brené Brown and Marc Brackett, business culture continues to move in a positive direction. For instance, lately, the idea of "safe spaces" is being discussed in workplace conversations, which is important because it recognizes the need for us to treat one another with more kindness and empathy. Once we are in an environment where set boundaries disallow offensive and dismissive words, then we can begin to positively contribute, affirm, and support people by building on the foundational tool needed for human beings to thrive: trust.

Although welcoming spaces of safety is a good start, Grace Space is about more. As we honor the fundamental right of human safety—both physically and emotionally—in an ever-increasing aggressive and violent world, we can also choose to be more proactive in bringing grace to our communities and places of work. Not only can we contribute to making safety a priority, especially for our most vulnerable and marginalized, but we can offer spaces that use open communication to build trust and create more humane spaces that bring out the best in all of us. This foundation of trust is needed not only for our professional lives but in our marriages and with our kids. Grace Space is an active intention to nurture deeper relationships with one another.

Success comes when the way we communicate with one another is more thoughtful, more constructive, and less reactive. For some this is a new idea, but it is not an impossible task. I'm hired by high-achieving leaders and fast-paced companies with hundreds of employees, and I've witnessed the practice of these tools and watched work environments transform. As well, I have witnessed how their transformed ways of thinking have also influenced their personal spaces in homes and relationships. Because when we choose to cultivate spaces of grace, it overflows into every area of our lives. We can create spaces of receptivity, connection, and trust. But it requires personal intentionality.

Extending grace means we practice thoughtful consideration, we give honor by our presence, we offer courteous goodwill, and we commit to being fair and honest. Every human is capable of offering grace, but if it were easy, we would all be doing it, right? We all want to be considerate, present, courteous, and fair. The challenge is knowing how to offer grace and having concrete ways to foster the use of grace in a given situation.

This book is about giving concrete examples for how you can foster spaces of grace where you live and lead by using these seven practices:

1. Responding vs. Reacting
2. Questioning vs. Accusing
3. Receptivity vs. Defensiveness
4. Constructive Communication vs. Destructive Communication

5. Connection vs. Protection
6. Freedom vs. Control
7. Trust vs. Fear

The purpose of this book is to support those who are committed to servant leadership rather than self-serving leadership. The iconic business consultant and author Ken Blanchard describes the difference between these two kinds of leaders:

> Self-serving leaders put their own agenda, safety, status, and gratification ahead of others who are impacted by the leaders' thoughts and actions. The shift from self-serving leadership to leadership that serves others is motivated by a change of heart. If leaders don't get their heart right, they will never become servant leaders. A misguided heart will color their thinking, impact their behavior and cause them to begin every day by asking, 'What's in it for me today?' That's certainly not servant leadership.[7]

Grace Space helps us get our hearts right as leaders—to serve those we lead in ways that call out personal potential while also achieving high results. It also provides for us a tangible way to invite those we lead to join us in a space that serves one another.

But let me be clear, Grace Space is not to be confused with passive or unresponsive behavior that excuses or

---

[7] Ken Blanchard. *Simple Truths of Leadership* (Oakland, CA, Berrett-Koehler Publishers, 2022), 6.

overlooks needed areas of growth. Quite the opposite. Engaging in Grace Space is about adjusting our own behavior where necessary. It is about actively creating a space where we tell the truth for the purpose of both personal growth and the greater good of the team.

The foundation that Grace Space is built upon is truth, trust, and transparency. But how we step into these needed conversations and the motivation behind what we offer are what is important. The seven practices around Grace Space provide the tools we need to get there.

The benefit of committing to cultivate Grace Space in the workplace is that it allows us to achieve higher results and with greater motivation and levels of fulfillment. More importantly, it serves our employees and teams by modeling to them how we can serve one another well. And as we do this, we raise the collective intelligence—both intellectual and emotional—of our teams and workforces.

We each have a choice to foster grace. When we stay mindful of how we live and work together, we create better spaces to accomplish more and serve humanity as it evolves into kinder practices. In choosing to respond with thoughtful consideration, doing honor by one's presence, and offering courteous goodwill, we commit to being fair and honest. Practically speaking, this yields higher results.[8] Together, in spaces of grace, we can achieve results that go beyond the bottom line, results that go after the human spirit.

---

[8] "Science Has Confirmed that Honesty Really Is the Best Policy in the Workplace," Entrepreneur. April 13, 2018. https://www.entrepreneur.com/leadership/science-has-confirmed-that-honesty-really-is-the-best/311011, accessed 12/18/22.

We have the power to hold welcoming spaces within us and between us. Grace Space is a welcoming space that starts from within and invites others to join us in the space between. May this book serve to help create a work culture that inspires others to join.

1. Responding vs. Reacting

Choosing to engage productively when we are tempted to retaliate; Choosing to understand when we are tempted to be right

We *are all connected, whether we like it or not. Let me explain* what I mean. Shawn Achor, a researcher on happiness, describes an experiment he conducted while waiting at a gate in the airport. He inserted an undercover researcher to stand within a five-meter radius of fifteen people who were waiting to board their plane. This person then began to bounce nervously in place while tapping his foot and anxiously looking at his watch with a frown on his face. Within two minutes, between seven and twelve of the fifteen individuals started imitating the impatient behavior, nervously tapping their feet and frowning at their watches.[9]

This is an interesting observation, but what I'm curious about are the three to five unaffected people. What made them ignore this behavior and not get sucked in? Maybe it's a complete lack of awareness. But could it be these few people have an inner resilience that helps them, when noticing the negative vibes, consciously chose to resist and instead stay positive?

I experienced something similar recently when grabbing a quick lunch between clients. Next to me were two young children acting out and two exasperated parents getting crankier by the minute. And other people were noticing too. I could feel my growing irritation at the young children and quickly realized that I was getting sucked into the negative vortex. So, instead of turning to give a cool gaze at the little offenders, I smiled and made eye contact with the parent as if to say, "No judgment here. I've been where you are and as much as we love these little guys, they can wear us out, can't they?" Then I looked at the little ones and grinned at them before turning back to my food.

It was a small act, and I'll never know if it made an impact on them, but I know it impacted me. Although I can easily react like the majority and show impatience, I thought of this study and remembered that I had a choice in how I responded. Rather than give in to the pull from two tired

---

[9.] Oprah Winfrey, "Shawn Achor: The Life-Altering Power of a Positive Mind," OWN Podcasts, recorded April 10, 2019. https://www.oprah.com/own-podcasts/shawn-achor-the-life-altering-power-of-a-positive-mind. Access date 12/1/22.

parents trying to enjoy their food as they felt the angry stares from other diners, I had a choice to respond in a mindful, more intentional way.

Controlling Our Emotions

When conflict rears up, we have a choice: we can respond or we can react. What's the difference? "A reaction is survival-oriented and, on some level, a defense mechanism . . . Often a reaction is something you regret later."[10] Reacting spreads negative stress and nervous energy, as the experiment in the airport proved. "A response, however, comes more slowly. It's based on information from both the conscious mind and unconscious mind."[11] Responding comes from a calm place where we remain fully in control and levelheaded. We feel the emotion but don't give in to it.

Here's what I mean. When I find myself getting irritated, I slow down to wonder why. Staying curious with myself, I get to the reason behind the irritation. For instance, it may be when someone is talking and I am confused, but they aren't checking to see if the listener is even understanding. They keep talking and I am getting more confused by the minute. I start feeling stuck in a listening posture. I need to get clarity and the longer it goes on, the more challenging it can be. I take notice of my irritation, and recognize it is confusion that lies behind it. My emotions are a flag, but I don't give in to the energy of

---

[10] "React vs. Respond," *Psychology Today*, posted September 1, 2016 https://www.psychologytoday.com/us/blog/focus-forgiveness/201609/react-vs-respond, accessed 12/1/22.

[11] Ibid.

the irritation. Instead, staying curious is the goal, which allows me to deal with the issue that lies *behind* the emotion—confusion. And since most of us really dislike feeling confused, (it's a common reason for anger, frustration, irritation, annoyance) I may hold up my hand or put up a timeout gesture so the person will stop talking, allowing me the chance to ask permission to get some clarity. Because to keep listening when I don't understand serves no one. I still want to keep the human connection, but also get the much-needed clarity. Here are some ways I can respond in this scenario:

- "I'm sorry, I have to interrupt you."
- "Hang on a minute, I need to back up and clarify something."
- Smile [this uses a nonverbal cue to diffuse] and say, "Have you noticed you've been on a roll?" (Humor can be a fun way to respond, not react.)
- "I can appreciate this is important to you."
- "I'm sorry, I've got to get going. Can we pick this up in our next conversation?"
- "Okay, I hear you. What do you want to do about it?"
- "Let me pause a minute and get this straight. I'm hearing you say _____. Did I get that right?"

So while I may have started out irritated, it's really confusion that lies underneath it, and knowing this allows me not to take it out on the other person. My irritation tells me something is off, so I cycle through reasons in my mind for why I'm having this response. Most people don't know how to take that second and stay curious about the "why." Sometimes the reason is as simple as "I'm hungry." Or maybe this is the third back-to-back meeting with the same company where I'm repeatedly hearing about the same issue. There's always a reason behind the emotion. Taking the time to get to what lies beneath is what allows us to respond versus react.

If I'm just hungry, it's not this poor guy's fault. I need to own that. The best action is to pause and stay calm . . . not suppress our emotions but choose to use them wisely. Emotions are important, they are trying to tell us something, so it isn't helpful to stuff them down. Instead, choosing to assert is a healthy response. For instance, is there one employee on your team who is always late to meetings? Do you wait for him or her to arrive before you begin, silently steaming? Here's a chance to assert in a healthy way: "Michael, you are a critical team member, but you have a habit of not arriving on time for meetings. If you aren't here when we're ready to begin the meeting, we will start without you."

On a more personal note, maybe you have an Uncle Frank who is always late to holiday dinners and your mom insists on waiting so everyone can eat together. Instead of letting frustration simmer along with the gravy, it's a great opportunity to assert a new approach: the rest of the family is here and the food is hot; let's eat and we can leave a warm plate in the oven for Uncle Frank.

In owning my emotional state for just a few seconds, I ensure it doesn't get projected onto someone else. I'm deciding how I can assert in a healthy way. Here are some helpful ways to remain in control in high-emotion situations—especially the hard ones like humiliation, sadness, disappointment, or betrayal—when tempted to react:

1. Stay curious.
2. Own your emotional state.
3. State what you want/need.

Surprisingly, responding doesn't take more energy than reacting; it can actually take less. It can be as simple as having a restful posture or making an effort to smile.

Let's take a closer look at what happens when we experience an affront. Our responses have an internal and external component to them—what we think and how we act. The connection between the mind and body is powerful, but we have the opportunity to use our God-given ability to choose what to do.

When the moment comes, the first response we have is usually emotional. We physically feel our annoyance or agitation. If we don't rein in our feelings, we can allow those initial reactions to become external. To practice responding, not reacting, the first step is to gain control of what we're feeling. If our first emotion is instant irritation, we may notice our blood pressure go up, our face get hot, our heart beat harder. The best course of action here is to hit pause. When we make a concerted effort to slow our breathing, it brings our heart rate back into normal range. Simply take a breath. Now take a deeper one.

The more you practice gaining control of your emotions, the easier it becomes to engage this control the next time. Dr. Caroline Leaf writes about the discovery of the brain's ability to create new pathways based on repeated behavior. We used to believe our brains, once aging and atrophying, were static. But our brain (physical) can grow and change based on how we think (metaphysical). This means we can literally change our minds about how we respond. We now know the brain has neuroplasticity, meaning it is moldable and growable. "Through using their minds, [patients] were able to change the physical structure of their brains as evidenced in their behavioral changes."[12]

When we are led by our initial feelings, situations quickly spiral out of control. But when we can stay curious with the reason for our emotions, we can address the external response with more clarity. We can choose to be positive. We can create Grace Space. This response then spreads positivity and reassurance.

I attended a three-day intensive speakers' retreat last year, during which the host showed us a video on the power of encouragement. A group of well-wishers got the names of all the runners in a local marathon. They divided themselves into groups and created signs with each runner's name. Then they organized gatherings so in the last quarter of the race, the runner would be cheered by random strangers holding signs and balloons. The video showed how the runners, unaware of what was about to happen, looked worn down and weary,

---

[12] Carolyn Leaf, ***The Perfect You*** (Grand Rapids, MI, Baker Books, 2018), 26-27.

but when they caught sight of their name on a sign and heard people cheering for them, suddenly their shoulders went back and their gait grew stronger. It was clearly a boost.

At the end of a three-day intensive, the host knew we were a bit brain fried from all the material we'd covered. So he arranged for a group of people to hold balloons and signs with our names while we were walking out to the parking lot to head home. When I saw the person holding a sign that read "Go, Heather, Go!" I felt like I'd just run a marathon. Somebody saw me and acknowledged how hard I was working in life. Such a small act meant so much. And aren't we all working so hard? Cheering one another on creates a space everyone wants to be part of.

Responding rather than reacting, while simple, isn't always easy. It can help when we are surrounded by others who are also committed to respond, not react. Here's what I mean. In a recent leadership coaching group, Andrea expressed extreme frustration regarding an employee on her team and an incident that had triggered a conflict. This normally calm leader was unusually emotional and knew it. In complete transparency, she stated that she was not in a good place to confront her direct report and asked the leadership team for help in responding to this employee rather than reacting out of frustration.

The group launched into action, offering ideas. The discussion afforded Andrea clarity to recognize something she'd failed to do. Andrea had heard from each member involved in the incident, but she had yet to speak with the employee who was causing the frustration. It was an easy ask that the whole team agreed on: Go get the employee's perspective. And sure enough, when Andrea asked her employee, she realized the conflict was based on a misunderstanding around job expectations, and Andrea was quickly able to clear it up with all involved parties.

Noticing when we're getting pulled into a negative space, and then pausing long enough to understand why we're feeling a certain way, allows us that split second to choose to respond rather than react.

Nonverbal Signals

Responding well also means understanding how we are communicating with our presence. Paul Watzlawick, the Austrian American family therapist, psychologist, communication theorist, and philosopher, created the Five Axioms of Communication, and he's most known for the statement that human beings cannot not communicate. He believed even our behavior itself is a form of communication.

Human beings are always communicating. We communicate in multiple ways—not only with words but in our tone, facial expressions, body language, and so on. Often, our nonverbal cues come across the loudest. "When there are inconsistencies between attitudes communicated verbally and posturally, the postural component should dominate in determining the total attitude that is inferred."[13]

[13.] Albert Mehrabian, *Nonverbal Communication*, (Abingdon, Oxfordshire, Routledge, 2007).

Research varies on how much our nonverbal signals make up our total communication—between 55 and 80 percent. Overall, it's safe to say the words we use matter less than the nonverbal cues we're communicating.[14]

Think how much we relay to someone we're speaking with when we offer a reassuring smile, a kind expression, curiosity in the way we lean toward them, or hope in our raised eyebrows and clear gaze. Just as easily, we can telegraph fear or frustration when we furrow our brows, show annoyance in a cool gaze, express fatigue in our slumped shoulders, or reveal defensive posturing in a flat expression and hard eyes.

Although it can be challenging for us as leaders to raise our awareness on how to respond well, the good news is that paying attention to our nonverbal cues helps a lot. Being mindful of this is a quick fix for how we can respond well simply by our presence.

Whether I'm looking at someone on the camera or talking to them face-to-face, when I see fear or confusion cross their expressions, it signals to me to slow down. Offering a reassuring smile goes a long way in shifting the conversation to better serve the person in front of me.

Here is a helpful four-step process for how to respond under pressure:

1. Slow it down.
2. Give clear context.

[14.] "Is Nonverbal Communication a Number's Game?" Jeff Thompson, PhD. ***Psychology Today***. Posted September 30, 2011. https://www.psychologytoday.com/us/blog/beyond-words/201109/is-nonverbal-communication-numbers-game. Accessed 12/1/22.

3. Be transparent, communicate clearly.
4. Offer hope.

Here is an example of how this may look in action. One of the responsibilities I incurred in my work with multiple companies was the tumultuous ride during the COVID season. Government mandates, vaccinations, mask wearing, and social distancing—these all became trigger words with the potential for dividing and generating fear, instead of unifying.

Keep in mind that often people react with heated emotions when the subject matter is personal, as was the case with many living in the pandemic when vaccination mandates, for example, jeopardized personal choice. Within a group of individuals, confusion can spread quickly. Choosing a healthy response can be hard when a person feels trapped or controlled. I know I struggle when anyone infringes on my personal rights and freedoms. Unhelpful reactions, however, such as pointing fingers, blaming, or shaming can lead to negative morale, distrust, fear, and, in extreme cases, conspiracy theorizing.

Conversely, leadership plays a role in modeling responsive, not reactive, behavior by not staying silent. Giving people updates goes a long way in helping to alleviate fear and uncertainty while respecting the employee's personal right to choose.

When we take the time to practice ways to respond consistently, we are better prepared to lead well under stress and in times of crisis. Our ability to be a "first responder" will come from clear, calm confidence. When we focus on serving the person in front of us, this helps us to lead mindfully and focus our leadership energy on best ways to respond rather than reacting in the moment. This is one way to create Grace Space in our environments.

Tips for Responding

- Choosing to respond rather than react slows things down to provide clear action steps and learning opportunities.

- Responding well doesn't mean you can't act quickly and decisively when needed.

- Remember the four-step process for how to respond under pressure:
    1. *Slow it down.*
    2. *Give clear context.*
    3. *Be transparent, communicate clearly.*
    4. *Offer hope.*

Practice Responding

Notice when you are responding and when you are reacting. Be intentional about slowing it down to buy you the time needed to choose a mindful response.

2. Questioning vs. Accusing

Choosing curiosity
when we're tempted to leap to assumptions

Think about *a time when you were accused of something. Or perhaps you were the one doing the accusing.*

I have been on both sides of this and neither one is fun. What does it provoke? In addition to surprise and confusion, we can feel instantly defensive. Worse, we lose the valuable brain power we need to problem-solve and come up with creative solutions because our brain goes down the path of whatever we practice. We can practice being accusatory and defensive, or we can stay curious and open-minded.

Before leaping to accusation, what if we asked the person why they feel so strongly about the issue? Imagine if we did that in American politics. Somewhere along the line, we lost our curiosity to ask the other person why they feel so passionately about a topic. What is more unsettling is that talking with people and hearing their perspective costs us nothing, but accusing them keeps us divided and stuck in an impasse. We've lost the ability to disagree and still care about each other.

I believe this is related to our need for others to validate our perspectives. What if we approached someone who takes a position that is opposed to ours and listened to them? Maybe what we're accusing them of isn't fully accurate. Our accusations are often based on assumptions. If we aren't looking for the other person's approval, then it isn't important for them to agree with us. Imagine the pressure that gets released when we go into a conversation with someone, not looking for them to validate or approve of our position but simply looking to gain an understanding of their "why." Curiosity is a dying trait that is critical to creating Grace Space.

If we're going to build bridges, we have to be able to sit down and talk—and listen—to one another. We are all members of families, work communities, neighborhoods, churches . . . we are all members of the human race. Instead of being able to sit down face-to-face and discuss controversial issues, we build camps and clubs with secret handshakes. I've witnessed how common this behavior is among religious groups, political parties, and even with personal values like how people may choose to raise their children or who they choose to marry. How much respect do we lose when we criticize others on their personal values and beliefs, which only serves to sow division and separation? I believe we can do better by creating spaces of grace where we stay curious about those who feel differently than we do.

When we step forward in Grace Space, we begin by taking the position of asking questions, not accusing the other person. Let me share an example of what happens when we accuse instead of question.

Gary showed up to our coaching conversation agitated. He had just come from an experience where he was ambushed by one of his employees. As Gary sat in his office, the door had burst open and this employee came in, arms flying, and accused Gary of passing him over for a promotion and undermining him with his team. Gary was so blindsided that he immediately began yelling back. It escalated from there. Gary knew there was a better way to handle the situation but was confused by what had happened. This is when we discussed the difference between accusing and questioning.

Had the employee poked his head into Gary's office and asked a question, such as, "Can I check something with you?" or "I'm confused about something and I feel it making me frustrated—can we talk?" it would have gone much better. As well, when we are being accused, we need to be prepared for how to respond so we don't mudsling accusations back and forth.

Here are a few ways to handle being unexpectedly accused. First, notice the confusion and surprise you feel and how it is pulling you to fight, flight, or freeze. With this realization, you are prepared to respond in some of the following ways:

- "I'm confused. Can we back up so I can better understand what's going on?"
- "I'm willing to listen to you, but accusing or blaming me doesn't help us get to a resolution. Can I ask some clarifying questions so we can discuss this together?"
- "I am feeling attacked and confused, which is only making me feel defensive. I care and value hearing your concern. If we can start there and listen to each other's perspective, I believe we can get to a mutual understanding. Can we start over? Or do you need some time to cool down?"

There are two sides to learning how to question rather than accuse: asking good questions and listening well. I'll explain. One day I received a call where the anger directed at me was palpable. Linden was angry that he was being "sent" to me for leadership development. Recognizing the feeling of irritation because of his accusations, I leaned into the conversation by asking questions that helped me understand where he was coming from.

Me: Why are you angry?

L: I don't think I should have to come to you. I already know what I need to do in leadership, and talking to you isn't going to help.

Me: I understand. I wouldn't like to be forced to meet with someone either. Have you ever worked with a coach?

L: No, but I worked with a counselor, and it was a terrible experience. She just kept telling me what to do and never asked me how I felt.

Me: I wouldn't like that either. Can I share with you how I work as a coach?

L: I guess.

Me: My hope is to understand where you are coming from and to know the challenges you face as a leader so I can serve you in developing the skills that will make your job easier and more enjoyable. Would that be of interest to you?

L: I suppose. But I don't want to be forced to do anything I don't want to do.

Me: Of course not. Neither do I. How about you get to say "stop" at any time in our conversation when it feels confusing or controlling? Then I'll pause and check in with you. Does that sound reasonable?

L: Yes. I would appreciate this.

And from there, we started a successful working relationship that lasted several years where we learned from one another as we tackled needed growth areas. As a side note, never once did he need to say "stop." Just knowing he was heard and had this option seemed to be all he needed. Asking clarifying questions that helped me better understand his frustration was important, but equally so was hearing him so that the next question provided further clarity between us.

If we want to foster this practice of Grace Space, we must learn that questioning is always the better route over accusing. And just as important as questioning is listening.

In my book *The Life You're Made For*, I share how we can engage in good question asking:

> The art of listening well is an acquired skill. Simply put, if the question inspires loving yourself and others better, then it is a helpful question. If a question influences self-hatred and bitterness for others, then the question is harmful. Asking the right question grounds our presence in this world.[15]

OES

When I start working with people, I ask three questions, which I call the OES, and I encourage the leaders I work with to do the same.

O: What are your objectives?

E: What are your expectations?

S: What would success look like?

As I listen, it helps orient me to better understand how I can meet the client where they are as we move forward to creating common goals. It also reveals the valuable information of knowing if we are on the same page or not.

When we as leaders start with questions, we meet people where they are in their understanding and perspective and create mutual understanding for how to move forward together. It also protects us from bringing our own

---

[15] Heather Penny, **The Life You're Made For**, (Self Published, Heather Penny, 2022), 40.

2. Questioning vs. Accusing

perspectives or agendas without understanding where the other is coming from.

Understanding how questions can either help or harm reminds us to take the responsibility and ask questions that encourage the trust to grow as we support individuals and teams in moving forward together.

Here are some questions to try out as the leader, which will help you find the clarity you need:

- OES—What are your objectives? What are your expectations? What would success look like?
- I heard you say _____ but I wasn't totally clear about the reason . . . Can you help me understand?
- What can I do to better support your role in the company and on the team?
- What feedback do you have for me?
- What do you need from me to help your job run more smoothly?
- Thank you for _____. I really appreciate how it supports my position. Can we add _____?
- I'm confused. Can you explain this to me?
- What do you think about _____?
- Would you mind if I clarified something?
- I appreciate what you are saying, but I don't have the time to respond, and I want to put some thought into it. Would you mind if I circled back around with you by _____?
- I'm curious about _____.
- Can you help me understand _____?

- Is now a good time to talk? I have a concern I'd like to discuss with you.
- We seem to see this differently. Can we talk about it?
- Can you tell me how your thoughts progressed in this?
- I care about how you feel and your perspective here. Would you mind sharing where you are coming from?
- Can I share my perspective with you?
- This is starting to get heated. Would you mind if we took a break and connect when we've had some time to think about it? I don't want to say something I might regret later.
- Do you feel heard?
- Is there anything else you need to make this a better working relationship?

When we keep an open mind, we get to solutions quicker. Try not to let emotions derail the conversation. If we can remain mindful of how we're feeling and, when we need to, take a short break to gather our thoughts, we can model what creating Grace Space looks like.

Tips for Questioning

- Focus on serving the person you lead by listening well and asking questions that show you care.

- Notice how you're feeling before you start questioning. Are you in a good place to listen well? Are you up for this conversation? Is now a good time to be able to hear what your employee is saying?

- It helps to have empathy for the employee's frustrations so you don't take anything personally.

- Sometimes we have to wait until our frustration at being accused subsides before we step into the conversation. It's okay to take a breather and circle around later.

- Don't be afraid to reach out to people who are equally committed to helping you form helpful questions.

Practice Questioning

Focus on asking good questions and listening well. Are your questions motivated from a place where you truly want to understand the other person's point of view, or are you asking questions to make your point? Be clear on your motivation when shifting the conversation away from accusing into questioning. This will allow you to authentically show up as you need to better understand what is going on and how you can help.

3. Receptivity vs. Defensiveness

Choosing to remain open and understand all perspectives when we're tempted to defend and reject

Do you consider yourself a receptive person? Do you welcome new ideas or new ways of looking at situations? Maybe you can relate to a recent situation my husband and I encountered.

Last year was a big year for me professionally because I launched my first book. My book-launch team had scheduled a book release party at my house, and I was excited but nervous. We planned to have a simultaneous virtual party so friends and supporters around the country could join the celebration online. While I knew I had earned the right to celebrate this milestone, the logistics of hosting were mildly stressful. On top of that, I was feeling anxious because writing a book is a vulnerable process, and I'm generally a private person. My life stories were going out into the world, and I was feeling intimidated by the public aspect of being "known" so well by strangers.

My husband of thirty years has been my best friend and partner most of my life. We had somehow gotten our dates mixed up, and he had an important conference he was scheduled to attend on the same night as my launch party. I wish I could say I immediately handled it with grace. I didn't. I was upset. I was stepping out into the public light, and I wanted my best friend and the security I feel with him. This conference was important to him, and while at first I was hoping he'd tell me he'd cancel the trip, I knew that wasn't the best solution. It isn't realistic to think he would be with me every time I needed him.

After a few days of simmering and then cooling off, I told him I was feeling hurt but accepted that I had to adjust my expectations. I was feeling insecure because I felt he had carelessly forgotten to mark the event on his calendar. When I chose to question instead of accuse, we were able to step into a conversation and hear each other's perspectives. It gave me the permission to set him free to decide what he needed to do and allowed me to then shift gears and get a few people in my corner who would help me feel supported in my feelings of high risk and vulnerability.

Learning to be receptive, not defensive, with our loved ones will give us the practice we need to exercise Grace Space with others. We have the highest expectations with those closest to us, and they can hurt us quicker than anyone else. This is another reason why it is important to hire coaches, counselors, or spiritual advisors. Getting wise counsel helps us understand the emotions we are feeling so we can stay curious and not swing into atmospheres that make us more defensive.

The following are some reasons why we get defensive:

- We don't feel heard.
- We have biased thinking (we've already made assumptions about the person).
- We're just plain tired.
- We lack trust with the person.
- We are confused and nervous that we don't understand. (Related to this: we don't feel qualified/we feel insecure in a situation.)
- It doesn't feel safe to ask questions.
- We are embarrassed by our emotions.
- We don't have the words to explain what we are feeling.
- We are unaware of our emotions.

How to Deal with Defensiveness

I've found the best way to deal with defensiveness is to talk about it. One of the biggest mistakes I see leaders make is not taking the time to talk with an employee to understand where their defensiveness is coming from. When we continue to allow defensiveness to go unchecked, it creates a toxic environment for the whole team that shuts down creativity and innovative ideas.

Defensiveness from a manager can become the culture that intimidates the team. As a result, people stop speaking up because it threatens the manager's ego. The manager has created a level of intimidation through their defensiveness. This is an imbalance of power. If managers are defensive, they are using their power against their team. On the other hand, if the manager is receptive, the team is more likely to feel heard and to function better. This is the essence of servant leadership. Receptivity unifies the team and propels them to move toward the same goals.

Many times, defensive posturing becomes a bad habit. Letting employees know that we value receptivity because it gets us to a place of mutual understanding can be a significant paradigm shift. Leading by modeling our respect for one another is a good place to start.

Speaking of respect, I want to tell you about Steve. I worked with Steve, a CEO and well-respected leader in his field, who was admired for his ability to empower employees to reach new levels of potential. In fact, I was impressed with his high-achieving team, and I wondered why he had reached out to me for help.

As we took a closer look, the reality was that some leaders were excelling and some were struggling. Most importantly, the company was no longer top in its industry and sales were consistently dropping, setting an alarming trend that Steve wanted to understand. Because of Steve's receptivity, we were able to assess the working culture in his company, which we discovered was "Being the best means doing it without help."

As I worked with Steve's executive leadership team, I noticed in them a nervousness about speaking up. Working independently had become a source of pride for this high-achieving group, and now no one felt comfortable speaking up to ask for help.

Honestly, I get it. Being able to do your work without help is rather satisfying. But it's unrealistic and doesn't work for the long term. Being able to work independently and know when to ask for help is an important balance to hold as leaders. It was time to integrate receptivity so the struggling leaders could get the help they needed and get back to excelling in their field.

As I worked with the executive team and the board, we started with the main issue of being receptive to the feedback employees and customers were trying to give them. Receptivity to the internal climate of their employees and the external climate of their customers became the new focus. The board encouraged Steve to lead the executive team in confronting the defensive culture that had dismissed much-needed feedback and in shifting into a culture that was willing to ask hard questions, listen, and stay open to input.

"Learn new ways and ask for help" became the leadership team's new motto. They learned from observing what their competitors were doing well. They started asking their customers how they could better serve them and were brave enough to ask where they might be dropping the ball. They modeled receptivity by asking managers what they thought needed to change and implemented some great ideas that increased both sales and morale. As well, they challenged middle management to get feedback from their teams in specific areas. The whole culture began to shift from a defensive one to a receptive one. And sales began to improve.

How do we foster receptivity as a leader? Think back to the Frankl quote from the introduction: "Between stimulus and response there is a space." We have a choice about how we will respond when faced with information we may not feel open to hearing. When we choose to create Grace Space, we act in a way that is fair, honest, and thoughtful, and that promotes goodwill.

Tips to Cultivate Receptivity

1. Affirm the Relationship—let employees know we value their desire to speak up and make the company culture better.

   - "Thank you for bringing this to my attention and for reaching out."
   - "I value your perspective."

2. Communicate Good Intent—even if we don't see eye-to-eye, we can still communicate our good intent. It is important to state this before jumping into our response.

   - "I want to hear you and ensure that we are learning from one another."
   - "I want to set us up for success and a strong working partnership."
   - "I want to understand your perspective."

3. Identify Target Growth Area (TGA)—this is where we, as the leader, share how we plan to grow from this new awareness. It might be a target growth area for us or for the employee or for both, because usually an area of growth connects to ways we can perform better.

   - "This was good feedback. Please share it with the team."
   - "Next time you aren't sure, please speak up in the meeting."

- "I'll make sure to circle back around with you. It sounds like I left you out of the loop."
- "I don't see the full picture; I'll need some time to investigate."

4. Set Clear Expectations—letting our team know what they can expect from us as well as what we expect of them helps keep the working relationship clear and respectful.
   - "Here's what I need from you, and here's how I will support you growing in these areas."
   - "Help me understand what you need."
   - "When were you hoping for resolution?"
   - "This is how we will hold ourselves accountable: set deadlines, give briefs on progress, and have check-ins to support growth."

5. Agree on Next Steps—setting clear action steps prevents any further confusion and supports an accountability process together.
   - "What do you think should be the next steps?"
   - "Here are the steps that will get us there. How do you feel about them?"
   - "If we commit to these together, ... "
   - "Let's agree on a date when we'll circle back around."

Practice Receptivity

Take the time to engage with the steps to foster receptivity. Notice how people leave conversations with you. Do they feel heard? Fulfilled? Affirmed? Inspired to grow and achieve? Focus on being approachable.

4. Constructive vs. Destructive Communication

Choosing to find common ground and staying solution oriented when we are tempted to cast blame and be cynical

For the sake of clarity, I have defined constructive communication as respectful, solution-oriented communication that values various perspectives in finding common ground. Staying constructive in our language requires a commitment. Who doesn't want to work on a team where they feel valued in their perspectives and unified in common ground?

Destructive communication, on the other hand, is when we blame, stonewall, accuse, dismiss, or use sarcasm. It is any form of communication that does not engage in a respectful, solution-oriented manner that values various perspectives in finding common ground.

It isn't difficult to think of examples of destructive communication. Don't we see this in our political parties? Imagine if we actually started focusing on what we have in common and stopped pointing fingers and blaming one another for the nation's problems. We'd accomplish much more because we would spend less time locked in power struggles.

It's worth asking the obvious question: If destructive communication is a lose-lose that keeps us from achieving results, why do we do it?

The following are some of the common reasons I have experienced personally, as well as reasons I've observed in my work with clients:

1. The situation is emotionally charged, and we don't understand our emotions or the emotions of others. Remember the example from my marriage? I was feeling emotionally charged because I felt vulnerable, and I wanted my husband present for my big event. But in the moment, I was not able to articulate that, because I was not in touch with how I felt. I was just reacting.
2. We're overwhelmed by our feelings (insecure, fearful, unsure, confused) and so the way we respond comes out messy. We attack, make assumptions, blame, shame, or guilt the other person.
3. Different perspectives make us feel uncomfortable.

4. It's a new experience, and we don't have the language to express what we want to say.
5. We feel vulnerable when we think we're out of our depth, and it scares us.
6. There's no guarantee for how this is going to turn out, so we power up to feel in control.
7. These uncomfortable emotions feel familiar to us, and we aren't sure what to do. For instance, *I feel ignored again. My dad did this to me growing up.* Or *I feel attacked, my last boss was volatile, and I never learned how to handle it.* This is the essence of feeling triggered.

Emotional Intelligence

Can you relate to any of these reasons for why we use destructive communication? I can relate to all of them. Do you notice how each reason has to do with emotional awareness? This is where our emotional intelligence (EQ) can help us out. The good news about EQ is that we all have it and experts have found proven ways to increase it. We communicate better when we understand what we're feeling, particularly when dealing with uncomfortable emotions like betrayal, sabotage, or disappointment.

Having a high EQ is about understanding what we feel and what the other person feels. If we walked around only acknowledging our own feelings, that would be narcissistic. We need to stay interested in what the other person is feeling as well. Sometimes we can lose balance, and that creates fertile ground for destructive communication. If we have a hard time knowing what we feel, we can't express it, and we lash out.

Dr. Marc Brackett, an EQ researcher out of Yale, states the importance of EQ in the workplace:

> We think of work as being driven by skill sets and information, by brainpower and experience, and by the hunger for achievement and accomplishment. All those things are in the mix, of course. But emotions are the most powerful force inside the workplace—as they are in every human endeavor. They influence everything from leadership effectiveness to building and maintaining complex relationships, from innovation to customer relations.[16]

Our EQs can help us understand why we communicate destructively, which in turn can help us find more constructive methods to implement. Linda's situation is a great example of this. She started working with me when she was burned out and frustrated. Fortunately, she had a supervisor who cared about her well-being and reached out for my help.

In our first conversation, it was clear to me why she was in such a state. Each team meeting brought with it inside jokes, subtle jabs at people's mistakes, and avoidance of the issues that were frustrating her. She realized in order to fit in, she had to keep her head down and figure out how to play the game to be part of the team. As a coping mechanism, she would isolate and work alone more than she should.

---

[16] Marc Brackett, *Permission to Feel*, (New York City, Celadon Books, 2020), 19.

4. Constructive vs. Destructive Communication

Although she had a caring boss, she had not learned to speak up about what was bothering her with her colleagues.

As Linda started to better understand her emotions around the work culture, namely discouragement, loneliness, and fatigue, she found her voice and went to her boss. He had missed the contagious, destructive communication that had been slowly growing around him. He hadn't noticed that not everyone was laughing. But as soon as Linda brought it to his attention, he was able to engage his EQ and lead the team, emphasizing his value for respecting one another's opinions and encouraging people to share without fear of receiving a sarcastic or belittling remark. All it takes is one brave person to speak up when a situation is destructive. The team leader then has a choice about how to respond: label Linda a "snowflake" and tell her she's being too sensitive, or comply and lead the team into more affirming forms of communicating.

Here are some questions we can ask that will help raise our EQ and foster more constructive language:

- What emotions am I feeling and why?
- Why does this feel familiar? (This helps us check the intensity level of our feelings. Are we more reactionary than normal? Have you ever thought, *I shouldn't be this angry*? This likely means it's a familiar, uncomfortable emotion. Try to identify when you've felt this way before.)
- How do I want to communicate my emotions constructively? (If you're stuck, think of someone you can bounce ideas off of who is committed to constructive communication.)

Remember, our EQ is rooted in realizing how we're feeling as well as how the other person is feeling. So the other half of this equation is asking these same questions of the other party as you seek common ground.

- What emotions are you feeling and why?
- Does this feel familiar to you? Is your reaction disproportionate to the situation?
- How do you want to communicate your emotions constructively?

Indirect Communication

Indirect communication can often be mistaken for destructive communication. Something as small as a sigh or grimace can make someone lose their nerve about approaching a hard conversation. A smile and thumbs-up can be just the encouragement someone needs.

We discussed nonverbal cues in section 1, but it is important to briefly mention the role nonverbal signals play in constructive and destructive communication. The best way to handle unclear indirect communication is with direct communication. If you aren't sure if a person means to be sending subtext, ask them! A kind way to address this is to slow it down and check in with the person without making assumptions. Stay curious.

Let's face it, we aren't always aware of the cues we send. I once asked a friend why he seemed to always be grimacing, and he laughed and said, "That's just my face when

I'm thinking!" Other times, these cues are meaningful and signal that a person is frustrated. As a leader, we can create Grace Space when we allow the person to speak and be heard. Sometimes it's simple and they explain, "I have a newborn and didn't sleep much last night." That lets us know today probably isn't the best day to implement a hard procedural change. But if they are frustrated at us, we don't take it personally; we stay curious. When we allow them to express what they are thinking or feeling, it is another form of grace.

Next time you find yourself in an emotionally charged situation at work, take notice if your verbal and nonverbal communication are aligned. I once worked with a leader who truly wanted to be approachable and hear his team's innovative ideas, yet when any of them reached out to discuss those with him, he responded with an exasperated sigh and a steely gaze that communicated irritation for being bothered. What he wanted and what he was communicating were incongruent.

When we worked together on this blind spot, he became conscious of his nonverbal behavior and began matching his intentions with his words by thanking them for reaching out. He even worked on his facial expressions in front of a mirror to make sure they communicated curiosity and care. Lastly, he readjusted his expectations. He didn't like to be interrupted in his workday, but he saw that was unrealistic. As the leader, his employees needed direction from him at times. He learned to structure his day with interruptions being a part of the job and scheduled important conversations so he could give his full attention. He was able to support his team and set up times for them to feel comfortable addressing important issues.

It takes work to find the words when we are emotionally charged. It takes integrity to match the words with our tone and nonverbal cues. As leaders we can have a no-tolerance rule on destructive language and model the way for our teams by using constructive communication and making an effort to ensure they feel seen, heard, and valued.

Tips for Constructive Communication

1. Never assume or accuse with nonverbal communication. Stay curious and ask:

    - "What's going on? I noticed you were sighing a lot."
    - "I want to pause here and check in with you because you keep rolling your eyes." (Try to use a tone that is compassionate, not aggressive. Be direct but with a soft touch.)

2. Commit to meeting people where they're at. Give them the permission to respond as they need to. If someone is emotional, they may or may not want to talk about it. Either one is fine, but have the courtesy and respect to ask.

3. Focus on what we have in common versus what we're annoyed with about them.

Practice Constructive Communication

Raise your self-awareness around your emotions as well as an awareness of others' emotions. Raise your EQ to better lead constructively rather than destructively. Make a commitment to be constructive in your communication and to confront destructive communication immediately.

5. Connection vs. Protection

Choosing to build bridges when we're tempted to build silos

As we commit to leading from Grace Space, we become more invested when we choose to connect with others. The practice of connecting calls out our working definition of "grace"—being considerate or thoughtful; doing honor or giving credit to (someone or something) by one's presence; having courteous goodwill or having a willingness to be fair and honest. These are all means by which we form connection with others. Choosing to connect with colleagues, employees, and other individuals important in our lives—many of whom we spend hours and days with each week—means being considerate, courteous, and present to them.

How our coworkers feel about us is important. Is there someone on the team we don't care for? Do you think that person senses that? Leaders tend to think they are more covert than they actually are, but it is pretty obvious how we feel about someone. And you can be sure the other person knows it.

So how can we move into connection with a person we aren't particularly fond of? It starts with holding the person who is in power most accountable. (The other person is held responsible, as well. They have to be receptive to connecting.) It's our job to stay curious around how to connect with our people. Here are a few starting places:

- Make it a priority to understand what they value.
- Hear their opinions. Truly listen to what they are saying.
- Learn what challenges they have overcome.
- Ask yourself, *Am I meeting them where they're at? Or am I meeting them where I am or where I want them to be?*

When we make this effort, it reminds us that our people are human beings, not just cogs in a wheel used to accomplish a goal.

In the Harvard Business Review boxset on Emotional Intelligence, in the book titled *Empathy*, the authors examined which trait was most effective in a leader, being lovable or being strong. "Most leaders today tend to emphasize their strength, competence, and credentials in the work place, but that is exactly the wrong approach . . . A growing body of research suggests that the way to influence—and to lead—is to begin with warmth."[17]

In leadership, we often look at who is the smartest or who casts the greatest vision, but research is showing us that humans respond more to kindness than aptitude. This doesn't mean we ignore competency, but it's telling us that warmth with competency makes for great leadership. It underscores how, at our most base level, everyone craves connection.

Jeff Weiner, CEO of LinkedIn, the world's largest professional networking website, describes in an interview the moment he realized the importance of leading with compassion:

> I vowed that as long as I was going to be responsible for managing other people, I was going to aspire to manage compassionately, where I wasn't necessarily trying to have [employees] do things the way I did them, but I would put myself in their shoes, understanding what motivated them, [know about] their hopes, their dreams, their fears, and try to lead as effectively as possible . . . Compassionate leadership begins with the connection between individuals. A company is comprised of the people; that's all it is. So when you are building upon a foundation of compassionate management,

---

[17] Jack Zenger and Joseph Folkman, *HBR Emotional Intelligence series.* (Boston, Massachusetts, Harvard Business Review Press, 2017) 39-40.

ultimately what the company is about, its vision, mission, its culture, its values, all of [it] is manifested in the way that its leadership is leading . . . the way the managers are managing. So, in that regard, managing compassionately becomes a bedrock of an organization.[18]

Raising our self-awareness of how we need connection and how others are trying to connect with us is related to our EQ. When we are aware of what we're feeling, we're able to connect authentically and meaningfully with other people. We're able to tell them we're sad, joyful, eager, disappointed. Wherever we fall on the emotional scale, the more we can understand what we feel and say it out loud, the more we are able to have meaningful connections.

People crave authenticity. We all know when we're not getting the truth or when someone is feeding us a line or playing mind games. I've worked with clients who are set on their own agenda, which distracts them not only from their own emotional awareness but from their teams as well. Because their focus is on their agenda, they honestly believe they are doing right by their team, yet they fail to notice that their team is miserable. The consequence of being treated this way is that people stop reaching out. They stop asking to be heard, or they learn to steer away from those who don't listen. This is true in whatever environment we're in, be it at home or at the office. These leaders aren't typically able to say how they feel,

---

[18] Oprah's SuperSoul Conversations. Transcript of podcast "Jeff Weiner: Leading with Compassion," recorded 9/3/18. https://www.podgist.com/oprahs-supersoul-conversations/jeff-weiner-leading-with-compassion/index.html at marker 8:44-9:41. Accessed 12/2/22.

so they may vilify anyone who crosses them or simply miss an opportunity to care for their team and perhaps redirect.

Do a check-up on your team and notice if you have people who have stopped speaking up, who are isolating themselves, or who don't seem happy. Grace Space keeps us solution oriented, keeps us moving forward, and keeps people who follow us inspired and encouraged.

When Connection Backfires

It doesn't matter how smart you are; if you don't have the ability to connect well with others, you will struggle as a leader. Maybe you're thinking, *I'm not interested in connecting with work colleagues; my job is to make the company money. I'll spend time connecting with others in my personal life.*

No doubt, connecting with others takes work, practice, risk, and personal responsibility. But we weren't made to do life on our own. When we stop engaging with people in healthy manners, we stop growing. "Research shows that collaborative problem-solving leads to better outcomes. People are more likely to take calculated risks that lead to innovation if they have the support of a team behind them. Working in a team encourages personal growth, increases job satisfaction, and reduces stress."[19]

What causes us to move into protection instead of connection? Perhaps we've been burned in work relationships. Maybe a colleague betrayed us, or we were promised a job

---

[19] "The Importance of Teamwork (as proven by science)," Atlassian, Worklife, posted 1/25/22, https://www.atlassian.com/blog/teamwork/the-importance-of-teamwork, accessed 12/21/22.

that was given to another person. Someone let us down, and now we struggle to trust others. We're just waiting for someone to betray, sabotage, or disappoint us. We have firmly determined to make life work on our terms.

If we think the world is not only against us but also not for us, we begin to tell ourselves that we're alone. This causes us to shoulder more and more responsibility as we single-handedly try to solve problems alone. Our internal dialog may sound something like this:

No one will help me.

Success is up to me.

If I want it done right, I have to be the one to do it.

To reach out for help is failure.

This is what leads us to slip into protection mode. The good news is, once we're aware of this, we can begin to foster connection by reaching out versus isolating and protecting.

Certainly, there are no guarantees in life; we know that, don't we? Sometimes situations backfire. The question isn't if but when. Fostering connection isn't about trying to solve the problem on our own, but rather asking, *Who do I want to invite in?* This choice allows us to build, not burn, bridges because we teach our people the value of connection and how it leads to success.

Don't get me wrong—there are times when working alone and having solitude are critical to achieve results. I'm talking about a repeated choice to avoid connection. When we do this, we not only fail ourselves, but we fail our people. We model to them that they can't reach out or connect, and they begin to feel isolated, frustrated, and alone. We want our people to feel the synergy, joy, and ease of healthy connection that makes them feel supported and want to get up each morning and come to work.

We have a choice in how we respond. It may take a while to bounce back from a situation that went sideways, but the key here is to bounce back! No matter how much life disappoints us, protection is not the answer. Choosing connection—with boundaries, with strength, and with wisdom—can allow us to be a student of life, to learn what we need to learn to become better leaders. And it makes it safe for our people to learn as well.

Connection is about giving people the permission to stay curious and grow. A leader's commitment to connection lowers the team's defenses and asks what they are learning and what they need to learn to get results. The very act of connection allows us to create that space of grace. To show up and not only offer our best but to become a better version of ourselves. The world needs the unique gifts that each of us has to offer.

Choosing Connection

Each person has the potential to cultivate a space and bring it with them as they engage with other spaces, be it Starbucks, a conference room, the golf course, or at the dinner table.

Recently I spoke to a group of nonprofit leaders—amazing people doing amazing things in our world. As the keynote speaker, I wanted to share the focus and build connection in the room. As I prepared, I realized my primary goal was to build as much connection from the stage as I could. So I opened my talk asking, *What have you heard people inviting in here tonight?* Words started flying—*compassion, hope, comfort, love, values, human dignity, abundance*—and the positivity in the room swelled.

Then I asked, *What are we rejecting as a group?* Words sounded, like *scarcity, poverty, isolation, confusion, chaos, despair.* This exercise reminded everyone in the room of their individual commitments and the collective commitment of the nonprofit to help those facing challenges. Emotion swelled in the room when we were reminded of the broken world we live in and how so many are struggling with financial, psychological, and educational barriers. We were rallying around our mission to do all we could to help improve people's lives. In a matter of two minutes, together we had created a heroic space that I never could have constructed from the stage on my own.

We, as a group, invited and rejected, using declarative words, what we were committed to. Although the room held a variety of over sixty nonprofit leaders, with unique mission statements and visions, we all united in our desire to address the human condition, specifically supporting fostered youths and at-risk children.

This is a great example of how we can deliberately and intentionally create the space around us and carry it with us. As soon as I walked off the stage, one of the audience members jumped up and hugged me. She said, "Thank you for offering sanctified optimism. We need more of this."

The most heroic thing I could do that night was make all of us the heroes. It is my deepest belief that it is in connecting that we will rise together as a human race. We have the capacity to solve world problems, and it starts in our little corner of the world. Lucky me that I had an audience to influence for ten minutes. If I had been living in a protective space, I would have focused on how I could be the hero. I'm my best as a leader when I can make it about the "we." I refused to let anyone make this about me. I was here to serve the room to connect us all in that space.

We have the personal power to shift the paradigm and offer words that are helpful, not hurtful; to collaborate, not divide; to offer safety, not blame; to offer healing, not wound. I propose a two-pronged approach: Create it and join it.

Create: If no one on your team or in your family is contributing to making the group dynamic positive, start modeling this yourself. You can begin a movement of cultivating Grace Spaces by forming new and deeper connections. What are you inviting in? What are you rejecting?

Join: People out there are already making connections—join them! Support their efforts, don't sabotage them. Foster what's already happening and help it grow. Find where you're needed.

A Practical Example

Over the course of our day, we make an endless number of choices. Maybe we wake up to a grumpy teenager and instead of being grumpy back, we choose not to engage with their negativity. We give them a hug or show them compassion, or maybe we simply hold our tongues and smile on the way out the door. Our goal isn't to be disingenuous with chipper comments and plastic smiles. Sometimes the goal is simply to not engage at their level. Thirty minutes later, we walk into work, and before we set down our bag, a colleague (loudly) confronts us about a situation. Instead of reacting, we say, "I really want to hear you. Can we set up a time to talk?" We are choosing not to give a frustrated response, and instead, put down a boundary and affirm the relationship. Once we are situated, we notice three especially hard emails in our inbox and it's only 8:30 a.m. We allow ourselves time to take a breath, refill our coffee, throw in our airpods, and play a happy song, something that resets us because it's not even midmorning and we have to do something to rescue the day. On the ride home, our spouse calls and asks us to go by the store and get some main ingredient for dinner. Instead, we offer another solution. "You know what? Why don't I pick up pizza?"

Notice how it is possible to create spaces that keep us in the driver's seat of life versus a victim of circumstances. This is how we can create Grace Spaces at the daily level and care for ourselves.

Connecting with Yourself

When I was on faculty, during breaks in the day, I would look for Grace Spaces I could join. But I had to be careful about sitting down to join my colleagues' conversations, because teaching is hard and it isn't easy to keep focus on building positive connections. It only takes one person to gripe about their students and it begins . . . Everyone has a story to share about an episode with a student that went awry.

Conversely, someone can share something remarkable or inspiring that a student did, and suddenly everyone wants to share a special student encounter they recently had. If I had a choice, (and we all have a choice, right?), I'd want to be sitting at the table that is lifting students up, not tearing them down, especially if I'm having a hard day. Not only do I want to be at the table lifting students up, but I want to be sure I'm initiating moments like these because I know all too well how easy it is to drift into negativity, which breaks down connection.

Finding Grace Spaces doesn't always involve other people. For instance, my introverted side really kicked in when I was teaching. Some days, the best thing for me to do on break was go to my own classroom and connect with myself. I would dim the lights, put on some classical music, and stay in the classroom to eat my lunch because I had nothing positive to offer, and honestly, I needed the rest. I learned this working in an office too. I've been part of a lunch group where I was the one who vented . . . Too many times have I wished I could go back and get a redo. But isn't that how we learn too?

Being in my classroom with the lights dimly lit helped me not resort to protection mode but stay in connection mode. It helped preserve my energy to stay connected with my students versus being exhausted from the day. I needed a break from conversation to refuel my body and mind.

Sometimes we have to protect our energy—protection isn't all bad!—in order to connect well. We can use our creativity and intellect to build bridges or use them to create silos. My hope is that as we continue to evolve, we spend more energy on building bridges.

Why We Protect

We don't have to work hard to achieve protective behaviors. It's easy to drift into spaces of blaming, unkindness, and shaming. When we're tired and disappointed with life, we can all slip into this. Environments can get toxic quickly. Silence, withdrawing, avoiding, arrogance, anger, biased thinking, marginalizing people, and racism are all forms of trying to protect our wounded souls or our tiny places in the world.

The person who is, for instance, sarcastic is someone who has (consciously or unconsciously) moved into protection because they may be fearful of putting themselves in a vulnerable situation. Just because someone has moved into protection mode doesn't mean they are bad people or naturally negative. I've had clients explain their reluctance to connect, and it often comes from an unwillingness to risk getting hurt or being disappointed by someone.

There is no way around it: Connection takes risk. It requires accepting the human condition and all that comes with it. Some fear the messiness that comes with this acceptance. We fear the process of connecting will take longer and make our job harder. We fear we'll connect with someone only to discover we don't get along. And some of us fear we don't know how to connect.

But here's another way of looking at it. Dysfunctional situations breed more unkindness and result in a dysfunctional culture. We must be intentional about changing the dynamics, whether at work or home. Maintaining a healthy connection is about keeping a balance of knowing when, where, and how to connect and when, where, and how to protect. It's okay if we don't get it right every time. Holding that balance between the two is what counts. Keeping in mind the context for all of this is grace, it allows us to explore meaningful connection and what each relationship needs to keep it healthy.

Brené Brown, a social researcher committed to understanding what supports us living wholeheartedly, defines connection as "the energy that exists between people when they feel seen, heard, and valued; when they can give and receive without judgment; and when they derive sustenance and strength from the relationship."[20] This is what keeps connections safe—helpful and not harmful. Taking notice of how the energy is working for us and not against us. True connection is about being seen, heard, and valued.

[20.] Brené Brown, *Atlas of the Heart*, (New York City, Random House, 2021), 170.

I used to own a coffee shop, and in the first several weeks, I had a huge learning curve. For someone who rarely drank coffee, it seemed as though, overnight, I was tasked with becoming a coffee connoisseur! One morning, I was filling in for a sick barista, but newly trained myself, I was a bit stressed. As the caffeine-hungry morning crowd formed, a growing line reaching out the door, my stress rose. I felt like I couldn't keep up, and I knew timeliness was critical for repeat customers. The stress must have shown on my face, because I heard a voice yell out, "It's okay, Heather! You're doing great!" To this day, I don't know who that kind person was, or how they knew my name, but I'm forever grateful. This customer not only chose connection with me but announced it to the whole coffeehouse, causing tension to leave the air as people shifted into rooting for me rather than resenting the wait.

See how connection can change everything? All I know is that it made me exhale and steady on as I methodically made one drink after another. It also made me grateful for such a small act with such a huge impact. I felt seen, valued, and heard. This is what connection does. And don't we all need that? Don't we want to lead this way, especially when we're under stress?

I'll share one more example. My friend once told me about a situation she found herself in when she was at the grocery store with her two-year-old and four-year-old. Their cart was half-full, and the four-year old was having a meltdown. My friend was at her wit's end, so she left her shopping cart and took both kids out of the store by their arms. As she made her way back to her car, a lady from across the parking lot, who was holding a child in her own arms, called out, "Hang in there, Mama!" Instantly, my friend described how she went from feeling desperate to feeling less alone. It helped to diffuse her frustration, and it built connection. My friend admitted how she sometimes calls out these same words to other moms who are struggling with misbehaving kids in stores and parking lots.

Connection definitely requires energy—but it also has the power to create energy as we derive sustenance and strength from one another. Wouldn't you say it's worth the risk?

Although these are personal examples, you can see how they would translate into the workplace. I have an executive leader client who often says, "I just need one person in my corner, and it's amazing what I can accomplish."

There's no easy formula for how to connect and no guarantee that the connection won't backfire. Sadly, because of this risk, some leaders opt out, choosing to focus on protection rather than connection. They lead from behind their desks, boardrooms, and organizational structure, not having time to "get involved" with their people.

Perhaps they get the results they want in meeting the bottom line, but the cost to themselves and their team is high. They have missed the opportunity to grow as a leader and as a human being. Worse, their people suffer from lack of the sustenance and strength that come from connection.

The leaders who choose to come out from behind their desks and who value building connection with their people are the ones making big differences.

How we show up day-to-day, intentionally choosing to connect in little ways, has a cumulative effect, like small deposits that eventually grow into a substantial fund. However, the reverse is also true. Choosing to protect rather than connect also adds up like consistent withdrawals draining a relational account, eventually breaking down trust and motivation between you and those you lead.

One of the "buts" I often get is "but I'm an introvert." I have a lot of introvert in me, so I get it. Really, I do. But it can't be an excuse for opting out. Rather, you get to lead in a way that honors your energy capacity for connecting. Here's what I mean. As a middle-school teacher, I would start each period with ten minutes of drawing and silence. I had read the research about how activating the right side of the brain increased learning, and I needed that time to regroup between each class. My introvert side was screaming for a pause before I jumped into another period with thirty-plus preteens.

As a coach, I lead retreats with a two-hour solitude lunch. After a morning of connecting, talking, and sharing ideas, I know we all need it, but honestly, I need the break in order to move into the afternoon session. When I speak or teach, I take the time to fill my energy tank beforehand with lots of alone time so I can have the ability to connect fully at the events.

In my daily work of coaching clients and groups, I make sure to build in margin times to give myself a breather.

Working with introverted leaders, we talk about noticing energy levels and what depletes. Having shorter meetings to prevent listening fatigue, doing walk-and-talk meetings to get a break from constant eye contact, building in margins for solo work time, and setting the necessary boundaries to be able to authentically connect are just some of the examples of how I build margin time in my day. See what I mean? Connection with people does not equate extroversion. Susan Cain, a researcher on introversion and author of *Quiet*, reminds us of the value of introverted leaders:

> But we make a grave mistake to embrace the Extrovert Ideal so unthinkingly. Some of our greatest ideas, art, and inventions—from the theory of evolution to van Gogh's sunflowers to the personal computer—came from quiet and cerebral people who know how to tune in to their inner worlds and the treasures to be found there.[21]

We need our introverts influencing the workplace. And we need our extroverts understanding the different rhythms introverts require in order to connect consistently and sustainably. Understanding what we need in order to connect well makes all the difference.

What If You're Rejected?

I have experienced the pain of reaching out and being rejected. And it hurts. I have witnessed this happen with many leaders as well. Sometimes when we try to build connection,

---

[21] Susan Cain, *Quiet*, (New York City, Crown, 2013), 5.

sadly, we get burned, and some leaders use this as a reason to move into protection mode. They resolve never to try connecting again, or they become super selective, only letting in one person.

I have also witnessed resiliency with leaders who refuse to allow their value of connection to be influenced, no matter how much they experience rejection. It takes tremendous courage to keep trying. These are unsung heroes. It is in these times that we're made into authentically good leaders. Will we allow the pain of rejection to form our values? Or are we going to allow it to grow us into resilient leaders? Not easy, I know. I speak from personal experience. But making the commitment is important. Find the people you need—coaches, counselors, guides, friends—to help you stay in the vulnerability of choosing connection. You will be proud of how it forms you and makes you into a person you want to become.

Choosing to accept the complexity over the simplicity of going solo takes courage. But from where I stand, it's worth it. It's worth the risk for the synergy that comes from working together. It's worth the risk for what I learn about being a better leader and, ultimately, a better human.

Tips for Connection

- Are you sending an email when a face-to-face conversation is needed?

- Do you avoid taking the energy to "walk the floor" or drop by personally to express gratitude and appreciation for a job well done?

- Are you taking the time to relate personally with your team by learning names of important people in their lives?

- Are you sensitive to an employee who is struggling by letting them know you "see" them?

- Do you let people know you value them and enjoy spending time with them?

Practice Connection

Notice areas where you are connecting with your people well and areas you might be avoiding. Step out of your comfort zone and try making new forms of connections that foster fulfillment and sustainability in the workplace.

6. Freedom vs. Control

Choosing to share power when we're tempted to dominate

I knew a leader of a prominent organization who was, well . . . powerful. But not in the way you would admire. Rather, he ruled through pressure and secrecy. He was known for secret meetings, unexpected terminations, handpicking favorites to advance, and unclear agendas. No one ever really knew what he was up to. Was he getting the job done? Yes, but it came from uncertainty and intimidation, which was how he controlled the culture in the organization.

His need to control became the loudest force in the organization. Innovation and creativity were not skills he fostered. He desired uniformity and didn't believe that each individual had something valuable to offer the team. People's respect for him was fear based. He was respected and feared versus being respected and beloved.

Here lies the difference between a leader who controls and a leader who trusts people with freedom. Don't get me wrong—having a structure and expectations is required in a healthy, functioning team. But we have to hold the tension between control and creativity so our work cultures can be influenced by new ideas.

Are we giving people the freedom to join our team, to come with their strengths and new ideas, or are we trying to control so much that we stifle the voice of the person whose natural, unique gifting could generate positive change for good? As a sidenote, do we know our team members' strengths? There are some great assessment tools out there that can support our clarity on the individual strengths of our people and how they can best be empowered to work as a team. If you haven't already, I recommend you have your team members take an assessment (i.e., Gallup's Clifton Strengths Assessment or Working Genius by Patrick Lencioni) and then be strategic in using the right people in the right areas for maximum impact and for their career fulfillment.

Leading with Control

I witnessed a recent example of what happens when we don't give our people the freedom to work within their strengths.

Alecia, a director, had learned about a new software that would help the company run more efficiently with greater accuracy and reduce turnaround times. Transitioning to this new software would also make Alecia's job, and the jobs of her twenty direct reports, much easier. The problem was, her COO, Liz, wasn't listening to her. But Alecia knew Liz's boss, June, the CEO, would love the idea.

Alecia approached Liz with the idea, but Liz shot it down, saying the current software was reliable and had served them well for the past thirty years. When Alecia tried to explain that the company had outgrown that system, Liz wouldn't listen. How could Alecia get the idea in front of June without undermining Liz?

By my recommendation, they formed a strategic meeting to discuss. Alecia got the idea in front of June, who was excited by the potential. June sensed Liz's reluctance and asked her about it. Liz's reticence wasn't only about change, but about the process of implementation and the time involved. She needed reassurance that she would be supported through the transition.

June took the situation as an opportunity to mentor both women. Liz's resistance was turned into a strategic rollout of the new software, which included training and extra support from the software company. It was a successful implementation, and the unexpected gift to all three leaders was that it allowed them to offer people more freedom and less control.

I like this example because there are no "bad guys." It shows how team leaders can offer freedom by opening lines of communication, and how control, often based on legitimate concerns, keeps progress stuck. Fortunately, it didn't turn into a power struggle but resulted in asking better questions regarding what would best serve the people and the company.

Control keeps things small. When we lead with freedom, it allows us to best serve our people and the company because we're asking the questions that are centered more around serving the greater good versus trying to control it. It's the difference in staying small and static and being innovative and dynamic. The latter is the best approach to serving our people. Nobody wants to be controlled. People want to feel they have the freedom to participate in a larger cause. Freedom is about inviting people to join you. Control is making sure they fit in within your agenda.

Controlling leaders believe

- they have to control to get results.
- keeping people under their control keeps things orderly; it's too high a risk to offer them freedom within the scope of their jobs.
- people cannot be trusted with autonomy.
- it isn't important for employees to feel free to create and be innovative; their job is to focus on the bottom line.

What are some reasons we might be drifting into a mindset that tells us we must remain in control?

1. We fear failure.
2. We lack clarity on what's best for the team/company.

3. We've stopped listening.

4. We've missed what the person is trying to communicate.

5. We lack trust in our people's abilities and skill sets. If we don't trust our employees, one of two things needs to happen: we either let them go or we help develop them. We might have missed how this person is in a job that is not in their wheelhouse.

Times of Transition

People might drift into the need to control others during a season of significant change. Transitions of any kind can trigger a fear of losing one's freedom. Change at work can generate uncertainty, often caused by a fear of being controlled by the new leader. Leaders must offer reassurance on why the changes are necessary and how the adjustments will serve the company by supporting growth, meeting customer demands, and ensuring more unity in the company.

If you are a leader navigating a time of transition and growth, offer employees Grace Space by incorporating the following suggestions:

1. Stay clear and consistent in your communication. Make sure your words and actions align.

2. Listen to concerns and give clear context. Offering people the freedom to share their concerns doesn't mean just listening without offering direction. It means listening with empathy, but then offering

context, guidance, mentoring, and direction that reassures them and gives them the clarity and confidence they need to make the right decisions.

3. Stay in charge of the narrative. Often during times of change, rumors fly. Make sure leadership is sharing an accurate narrative and recognize the message may need to be addressed repeatedly.

4. Proactively ask for input and insight. Employees have a unique perspective that executive leadership doesn't have. Make sure teams feel the freedom to share their observations because it raises the collective intelligence in the room.

5. Remind everyone of the important role they play in the company. People know if they are valued and if they aren't. Especially during seasons of change and growth, communicate the value each person brings to the team.

Freedom Is Grace

Ultimately, the degree to which we extend grace relies on how much freedom we offer one another. Offering freedom, not control, is essential in showing a person their value. If we are going to be people who provide spaces of grace, then individuals need freedom that is inspiring and motivating to them. When we offer them freedom, we are saying, "You count. I see you. I value you and what you bring to the table."

Ken Blanchard wrote, "People don't resist change; they resist being controlled." The servant leader is focused on helping team members reach their potential and achieve goals, not on micromanaging them into obedience.

Blanchard describes servant leaders as people who lead by

- sharing an inspiring vision on where the leader is taking his or her people;
- communicating clear direction and what it means to achieve success;
- involving their people in setting the course for the organization and determining desired results;
- taking responsibility for when employees do not have clear direction on how to achieve results;
- creating partnering relationships with their people to achieve clarity around direction to ensure everyone is on the same page;
- shifting to serve people by setting clear goals and coming alongside to support accomplishing them once clarity around vision and direction has been established;
- reassuring people about the role of leaders being to serve them in achieving goals through training, resources, and clear communication.[22]

Notice the freedom that comes from servant leadership. No secret meetings or confusion around agendas and goal setting, but open communication that is focused on building trust and setting people up for success. With transparency comes freedom.

[22.] Blanchard, *Simple Truths*, 118.

Many organizations today seek to create a business culture of innovation and out-of-the-box thinking because their industry depends on it. They don't have the luxury of staying status quo. Google, for instance, offers flexible workspace, free food, and casual dress—perks that are typical for many tech companies. But Google is one of the few who designed their building to include:

> [a] labyrinth of play areas; cafes, coffee bars and open kitchens; sunny outdoor terraces with chaises; gourmet cafeterias that serve free breakfast, lunch and dinner; Broadway-theme conference rooms with velvet drapes; and conversation areas designed to look like vintage subway cars . . . Everything has been researched and is backed by data. In one of the open kitchen areas, Dr. Welle [a "people analytics" manager who has a PhD in industrial and organizational psychology] pointed to an array of free food, snacks, candy and beverages. "The healthy choices are front-loaded," he said. "We're not trying to be mom and dad. Coercion doesn't work. The choices are there. But we care about our employees' health, and our research shows that if people cognitively engage with food, they make better choices."[23]

This work environment and others like it are championing the unique skill set and creative energy each person brings. They are giving their employees the dignity of respecting their free will and the value they bring.

---

[23] Charles Duhigg, "Looking for a Lesson in Google's Perks." *New York Times*, posted March 29, 2015, https://www.nytimes.com/2013/03/16/business/at-google-a-place-to-work-and-play.html accessed 12/23/22.

There is a local hospital in my hometown that has adopted practices that telegraph to patients that they are more than just a body or a room number. They ring a bell that sounds across the entire hospital whenever a baby is born. They keep four full-time chaplains on site to help with the spiritual well-being of their patients and family members. They offer support groups for parents who have lost children.

Someone in that organization had the influence and presence of mind to remind their employees that they were dealing with real people—the sick and dying as well as new life being birthed, all of which deserves to be acknowledged with respect and dignity. This is how we honor the free will of the individual. We give them the freedom to respond to their emotions. Seeing the whole person—made up of body, mind, heart, and spirit—is a necessary component of creating Grace Space.

One final example of how we can honor the freedom of our humanity instead of trying to control it . . . There is a veterinarian that has a candle at the front desk with a sign that reads "If this candle is lit, please stay quiet as someone is saying goodbye to their pet." They aren't trying to control another's emotions, but instead are honoring it. They chose to signal to others that there's a painful, heartbreaking event happening. I don't know about you, but I would want to know when another human being is facing a challenging and painful time so I can have a sensitivity that supports that human being. Joining people in their time of need and being sensitive to what they are facing makes us more humane.

When work cultures grapple with honoring the freedom of our humanity, versus trying to control it, we create Grace Space.

Freedom allows us to think for ourselves, to offer our best self, to better understand each other as we watch how each person offers their gifts to the team, and it reminds us how unique we all are—we aren't robots that all fit in the system the same way. When we can recognize potential and call it out, we motivate people to want to serve the greater cause of the group because they know what they have to offer is valued. Grace Space is about valuing the individual and supporting their value in the team as a whole.

Tips for Fostering Freedom

Questions to ask team members:

- What would make your job better? Easier?

- What are some changes you see that could best serve the company?

- What is your team asking you for that we could support you in giving them?

- What ideas would you like to bring to the table that could best serve your people?

Practice Freedom

Leading with freedom is about inviting people to join us—not forcing them to follow. So, how do we inspire people to join us as leaders and still yield high results?

- Give clear parameters around job responsibilities and then set them free. Create clear boundaries and teach people to do the same around job responsibilities and communication so people can work autonomously in their areas.

- Mentor our people in where they are going and the best way to get there, partnering with their authentic style.

- Communicate appreciation of them and the role they play on the team. Continue offering guidance and direction where necessary.

- Understand who they are and what fulfills them, affirms them, and where they want to grow and achieve.[24]

- Identify their potential and continue calling out where they can be successful. Support learning from mistakes.

- Celebrate wins, successes, and met goals.

- Make sure the right person is in the right conversation talking about the right thing. Before the meeting is set, ask: Is everyone present who should weigh in on this? Is this the right time to be scheduling this? Do we all agree on the same objectives? Are we all on the same page with the needed results? Have the objectives been clearly defined?

---

[24] I call these the Four Tires (see chapter 14 in my book *The Life You're Made For*)

7. Trust vs. Fear

Choosing to believe when we're tempted to panic

I left talking about the practice of trust versus fear for the end of the book because it is the one I hope stays with you the longest when you've finished reading. In many ways, trust is the very foundation for the idea of Grace Space.

Patrick Lencioni, business expert and author of eleven books, has a similar view of trust. In his book *The Five Dysfunctions of a Team*, he identified the five root causes behind teams and companies underperforming. In the shape of a pyramid, he listed from top to bottom: Inattention to Results, Avoidance of Accountability, Lack of Commitment,

Fear of Conflict, and—at the base of the pyramid—Absence of Trust.[25]

Why is trust so foundational to the health of the team? Because when leaders lack trust, they become defensive, fearful, and—most destructive—they stop believing in the goodness of others.

Let me ask you a question. What does your internal landscape look like when it comes to trust, especially when things don't go well? Do you trust yourself? Others? The process?

Let's imagine we put on ten, fifteen, twenty extra pounds. The natural reaction would be one of fear. Fear that we won't be able to lose the weight. Or that we'll lose it and then put it right back on. We fear not knowing who to listen to—no carbs or no sugar? This fitness guru or that one? This starts up an internal dialog of fear. You might have paid for the fat-loss pills or hired a trainer, but what is motivating you is fear of not getting it right or not being enough.

I'm going to share with you one of the most powerful stances we can take in this life. Imagine the next time something bad happens that you respond with these thoughts:

> *I don't know the answers yet, but I trust myself, and I trust the process. I trust the right person will come and offer me support. I trust the right knowledge will come across my path. I trust I'll know what to do when the moment comes. I trust it will all work out.*

---

[25] Lencioni, **The Five Disfunctions of a Team.**

Now, let's put that in the context of leadership development. When we make a mistake, we might be tempted to tell ourselves, *I'll never do that again. That's the last time I take that risk or let myself be vulnerable.* And certainly, there may be some truth we learn that helps us not repeat mistakes, but more often than not, we can allow fear to become the motivation for why we don't risk again, or trust people.

I mentioned earlier that I once owned a coffee shop. My husband and I took a leap of faith and ventured into the coffee business. It ended up being something we really enjoyed—for the first few months. Turns out, I don't like working with food, managing employees, making schedules, dealing with vendors, buying products, or being responsible for a venue—all things necessary for running a coffee shop! Although we were able to sell it within two years, I found myself a bit insecure about embarking on another business venture. How did I miss it so badly and not recognize what I would like?

See what I mean? When we encounter a significant failure, it can be easy to mistrust ourselves again. If we don't learn to trust ourselves, we won't trust our people. We usually grow an internal dialog of fear because of one action that backfired. Then that fear is fed and grows. We lose our trust in people, in ourselves, and in the process. We forget that humans need to be nurtured because the culture tells us any and all action is a threat.

We remedy this by learning how to hold the tension between trust and fear.[26] Learning to see the coffee shop as

---

[26] If you're interested in learning more about this, I devote an entire chapter on "Holding Tensions" in *The Life You're Made For*.

a valuable learning experience, one that taught me what I don't like doing, eventually led me to start my next business—a coaching company with no food, no employees to manage, and no venues to upkeep. When we choose to trust the learning process, we lead by modeling. We help our people trust the learning process as well without creating fear-based policies where we feel pressured to lead from a position of perfection that states, *We cannot get it wrong*.

Here are the four main reasons that trust breaks down:

- Suspicion
- Secrecy
- Sarcasm
- Hypocrisy

When we have an internal dialog of suspicion, it leaks onto our thoughts and actions—and before we know it, we are leading defensively. Defensive leadership makes people nervous; it makes them feel disconnected, insecure, and unsure of themselves. Fear causes leaders to lose the human connection.

We are afraid of enduring the hard experience again. Instead of deciding to learn from our mistakes, many of us make a vow of security. This vow is dangerous because it can lead to selfishness. When we focus too much on our need for security, we miss out on what others need.

The reality is, when we put ourselves out there, it doesn't always go well—whether it is with our team at work or with an old friend. But we all have a choice. We can build a wall around ourselves (or our team, or our family, etc.) or we can trust that, while we may get rejected again, we can trust ourselves . . . we can trust others . . . we can trust the process. The right person or advice or insight will come.

I was recently listening to a podcast where a popular spiritual leader shared how he had gotten a black eye. He didn't share the details, but this man is well known for working with young men in prisons. My ears perked up when he said he wouldn't stop going to the prison. He wasn't dissuaded from the mission he had to reach hearts. Best-selling author and speaker Bob Goff is another example of this. The villains of the story get love too. We don't stop because someone rejects us or betrays us.

So many more are waiting to be reached with the message you're carrying. Don't let one person spoil the riches of what you have to offer the world.

When I was starting out in my career, I got asked to participate in a speaking opportunity. I didn't know my audience. I didn't do my homework. You see where I'm going . . . I'm embarrassed to say I bombed. I stood onstage, soaked in my humiliation. After that, I told myself I wasn't made to speak. I'm grateful the story didn't end there. I had some trusted friends who insisted it was a one-off and that I'd never make that mistake again. They encouraged me to find the learning experience in it. It took some time, but I slowly learned to trust myself and was able to say, *You got it wrong, and it's going to be okay. You are made to speak, and you're allowed to get it wrong and learn from it. You get to trust that people will forgive you. And even if they won't forgive you, it's still okay.*

We all have permission to learn in life. This is where trust grows. We're all students learning how to show up and put our best foot forward every day. Life is a classroom. If we stop trusting, we become the student in the back of the class with the hoodie covering half their face. If we give our leaders permission to lead with defensiveness and fear, they're no better than the kid at the back of the class, hiding from the world.

Here are some suggestions if you struggle with trust.

One, have trusted advisors—a.k.a. failure experts—in your corner who have grappled with their own fear and have refused to let it take them out. There is a resiliency in them that you can emulate. Everyone messes up badly, several times in life. The way I faced that was by getting comfortable with messing up. Don't get me wrong—I don't enjoy it. But we can live paralyzed by the fear of messing up, and it becomes a self-fulfilling prophecy because we were so rigid in avoiding it. I got to where I could take a deep breath, try to relax, and tell myself, *What could I do that would be so bad that I couldn't recover?*

I keep people with a high level of discernment close to me. They help me get prepared to be my best. I have a team around me. Go to people and ask for their help to recover from fear-based thinking. Tell them, "I don't want this to take me out, and I'm afraid it might." Get rid of fear advice-givers who encourage you to flee hard things. That will never bring you peace.

Two, do your growth work. The best gift we can give our relationships and our world is to do our growth work. Face your demons. What are the things that keep you up at night? Ask yourself, *What am I scared of?* Deal with the harder stories that are holding you back first. You get to trust that the right people will come across your path. If you're living in fear, you aren't looking for those people, so you're probably missing them. Friends, coaches, teachers, counselors, spouses, family members, pastors, our children. We have so many guides in this world who want to support us in building trust.

Three, don't trust naively. This isn't about rainbows and unicorns. Life is challenging and confusing at times. Disappointment and betrayal abound. Make no mistake, I understand how trust gets weakened. It's the brave who say, "I won't let this take me out—I don't know how, but I'm committed to that," then make sure they have someone in their corner.

Four, don't give fear a place to roost. Fear backs us into a corner. If you keep living in a place of distrust, there's a high chance you'll be lonely. You can water the tree of fear or you can water the tree of trust, but have no doubt, one of them is growing in you. With the tree of fear, the ultimate act never ends well. Fear is very isolating; trust is connecting. Fear hides; trust is transparent and authentic.

As leaders, we are influencers. We send the message; we set the tone. When we fear as a leader, our people fear. When we fear as a parent, our children fear. When we feed dark thoughts, they create and strengthen a pathway in our brains. We may not catch the dark thought before it comes, but we can choose to follow it up with a positive thought.

Start by believing there are people to connect with who won't betray us. Once we believe that, we then can start looking for them.

Fear-Based Leadership

Managers who incite fear in their team members are drawing from a well of their own insecurities. Fear not only tears down trust but also turns the relationship toxic. It breeds doubt, suspicion, and insecurities. We have many historical examples of leaders who used fear to manipulate the population—Hitler, Mussolini, and Stalin, to name a few. Cult leaders like David Koresh and Warren Jeffs used fear to control their followers. These are extreme examples, but milder and less destructive forms of fear management occur every day. Some leaders prefer email and speaking behind a podium because they fear one-on-one encounters could lead to being publicly challenged by colleagues.

To enforce their power of influence, the fear-based leader may:

- Manipulate
- Threaten
- Coerce
- Exclude
- Intimidate
- Publicly humiliate
- Withhold key information

Trust-Based Leadership

Holding fear creates shame spaces. We can hold either fear or trust, but we cannot hold both. Grace Space doesn't work without trust.

Trust-based leadership recognizes when a person or group is unfairly being excluded or marginalized and does something about it immediately. I witnessed an organization knowingly marginalize a group of people for years by preventing them from participating in leadership based on gender. Even though it was identified and talked about, it wasn't until over two decades later that the leadership addressed it. But by then, the harm that had been done in both the organization and the community they lived in was costly. Their reputation as an organization that excluded certain people based on gender had broken trust with people everywhere. It was hard to watch the damage it had wreaked due to the slow response rate of addressing a serious and toxic issue that was hurting people.

On the other hand, I have a client who is the leader of the company and such a positive force on her team. She loves a challenge. It's inspiring to witness. Here are some things I've overheard her say to her team:

That is a problem; let me think about how to help you.

We'll outsource that.

I trust in your ability to handle this well.

We'll get you the support you need.

I trust you, and here's what I'll do to support you.

Don't worry if you don't have the vision. I do, and I'm here every step of the way.

I will be getting involved, not because I don't trust you but because I believe we are better together and we need one another on this project.

She offers reassurance because she trusts the leaders. When she needs it, she consults with trusted advisors to get input and insight.

One of the gifts that comes with trusting our team is the benefit of collective intelligence. Leaders who are fear based hold their cards close to their chest because they don't trust the room. This tactic doesn't allow collective intelligence to sync up and grow in a room. Think again of the atmosphere Google set up with open work spaces and dining options where colleagues could gather and talk.

I've had many clients come to me because they want to be a better leader, but they won't show their cards. They hold them close to their chest, causing confusion and suspicion. We can't address a dysfunctional team without being transparent. Transparency is what builds trust. Build trust at all costs, because organizations leading without the emphasis of cultivating trust is like a house of cards ready to fall at the next misunderstanding or big fail.

Earning Trust

How do we inspire trust in our people? First, we must recognize that building trust is not a switch to be flipped but is on a continuum. It can increase and decrease based on our interactions. It is important to keep a pulse on it to assess whether trust is growing or shrinking.

We should never assume where the trust level is with another person. Instead, we observe, ask, and stay alert to the trust level we have with each person and the group as a whole. When trust needs strengthening, be generous in giving credit where credit is due when things go well, and be quick to take responsibility when things don't go well.

Trust is the heartbeat for Grace Space. We need to trust in our own ability to create Grace Spaces and invite our people to join us. Putting trust into action means leading with transparency, reaching out to initiate trust-building conversations, and sharing our knowledge with the belief that we are better together.

Restoring Trust

- Recognize when trust has been lost. At times, we land in a situation where we lose our trust with someone. The first step is in recognizing when trust has been broken and doing what is necessary to restore it. Share responsibility for the damage caused and let them know what you learned; ask them what they learned and agree on a plan to repair it. Make it a win-win and keep the feedback door open as you set a new course together.

- Circle around consistently. Check in and find out what's behind the mistakes. Is it lack of training? Personal life is in crisis? Lack of support or resources? Lack of direction? Or is it sheer lack of taking responsibility for their actions? Find out what's going on and do something about it that meets the person where the issue lies.

- Build trust by getting to know them through their Four Tires of Fulfillment, Affirmation, Growth, and Achievement. I call these the Four Tires because they need to be checked regularly, and if any one of them is low or even flat, it can cause us to lose traction and get stuck. As leaders, it is important to keep a pulse on our people by asking about their tires. What fulfills them? Affirms them? Where do they want to achieve and grow? We foster trust when we find out about our employees, and when we are transparent with them regarding who we are as a leader.

Having a team that trusts one another and trusts their leader is the basis for being able to achieve high results. It also cultivates a healthy work culture where people want to come to work and do their best for the good of the company.

Trust is about cultivating spaces that give us each permission to show up with our authentic selves. It communicates value and recognizes each person as an important member of the team. This is the essence of Grace Space. Fear puts up walls that prevent Grace Space; trust tears down the walls.

This chapter is my callout to leaders to commit to trust building above all else.

Tips to Grow Trust

- Emphasize the importance of collective wisdom rather than working solo.

- Recognize and communicate the value each person brings to the group.

- Set clear OES —define the Objectives, Expectations, and Success. Make sure no one is confused about where the team is heading. I have seen this break down trust quicker than any other bad habit in leadership. Unclear definitions around objectives, expectations, and success erode trust and allow space for confusion to take root. Providing clarity around your team's OES is a natural and strategic way to build trust with your people as well as model to them how to build trust amongst themselves. When trust is cultivated, people's morale goes up. And don't we need more motivation and fulfillment in our places of work and home? It all starts with trust in our spaces of grace.

Practice Trust

Take a "Trust Inventory" in your own life. Where do you trust yourself? Where do you struggle to trust yourself? What happened that made you skittish about trusting yourself? Create a plan to address this. It might mean involving a coach, mentor, counselor, or trusted friend who can help you.

Tell your people (or any relationship you care about) that you are committed to building trust and want to know what they need to do this. Keep the conversation open and check the trust continuum to see how the relationship is doing.

Remember that we don't drift into cultivating trust in our relationships. It requires intentionality and purposeful evaluation.

The Wrap-Up

We have the tools we need to make a huge impact ... in our lives, in the lives of the people on our team, and in the world. Now we have a choice to make. We can be a positive voice in the world or join the voices that seem to thrive on the negative.

Before you dismiss this as a foregone conclusion, commit to doing the work necessary so your leadership comes from a place of wholeness: body, mind, heart, and spirit. Leadership begins within, and I don't believe we can divide how we live from how we lead. We can't fragment who we are into parts and only address our "work selves." We lead from who we are, and who we are is complex and interconnected. Let's model to our people the importance of taking care of all the facets of ourselves so we can bring our best selves to our work.

Together, we can do this. Let's be about creating a space centered around responding with thoughtful consideration, doing honor by one's presence, and offering courteous goodwill with a commitment to being fair and honest. Don't we all want this? In an increasingly angry and violent world, I crave it. Grace Space is how we start.

The cover of this book shows a tree with its roots going deep down into the soil. Did you know that the roots of a South African wild fig tree can go down as far as 390 feet? Amazing! The roots are what anchor the tree so it is stable against the wind and the weight of leaves in the summer and ice in the winter. Roots feed the tree. It is also the roots that allow trees to communicate with one another as well as share water and nutrients.[27]

How far down do your roots go? What do you pull from to anchor and feed you? We all have roots growing somewhere. What are your roots growing down deep into? Do they grow in soil that is conditioned with responding, questioning, receptivity, constructive communication, connection, freedom, and trust? Or is your soil fed with reacting, accusing, defensiveness, destructive language, protection, control, and fear?

As leaders, we have the power of influence; as humans, we have the power of choice. My hope for myself, for you,

---

[27] Based on research from **The Hidden Life of Trees** by Peter Wohlleben.

and for all the world is that our roots go down deep into the soil of grace.[28] In doing so, we will be creating spaces of grace wherever we go. And people will be drawn to this. Grace Space is synergistic. It only takes one person offering it before others are drawn to it and join it. I have watched it happen over and over. Be that person.

Now, I want you to imagine me holding up a bouquet of balloons and a huge sign with your name on it, jumping up and down and cheering you on as you begin your journey of bringing positive change to your places of work . . . to your homes . . . and to the world.

---

[28] Reference Ephesians 3:17

Bibliography

Blanchard, Ken. *Simple Truths of Leadership*. Oakland, CA: Berrett-Koehler Publishers, 2022.

Brackett, Marc. *Permission to Feel*, New York City, Celadon Books, 2020.

Brown, Brené. *Atlas of the Heart*. New York City, Random House, 2021.

Cain, Susan. *Quiet*. New York City, Crown, 2013.

Duhigg, Charles. "Looking for a Lesson in Google's Perks." *New York Times*, posted March 29, 2015, https://www.nytimes.com/2013/03/16/business/at-google-a-place-to-work-andplay.html accessed 12/23/22.

Entrepreneur. "Science Has Confirmed that Honesty Really Is the Best Policy in the Workplace." April 13, 2018. https://www.entrepreneur.com/leadership/science-has-confirmed-that-honesty-really-is-the-best/311011.

Frankl, Viktor. *Man's Search for Meaning*. Boston, MA: Beacon Press, reprint 2006.

James, Matt, PhD. "React vs. Respond." Psychology Today. Posted September 1, 2016 https://www.psychologytoday.com/us/blog/focus-forgiveness/201609/react-vs-respond.

Leaf, Carolyn. *The Perfect You*. Grand Rapids, MI: Baker Books, 2018.

L'Engle. Madeleine, "Madeleine L'Engle Biographical Sketch / Page 3 of 4." Accessed 12/20/22. https://www.madeleinelengle.com/madeleine-lengle/madeleine-lengle-biography-3/.

Mehrabian, Albert. *Nonverbal Communication*. Abingdon, Oxfordshire, Routledge, 2007.

Oprah Winfrey, "Shawn Achor: The Life-Altering Power of a Positive Mind," OWN Podcasts, recorded April 10, 2019. https://www.oprah.com/own-podcasts/shawn-achor-the-life-altering-power-of-a-positive-mind.

Oprah's SuperSoul Conversations. Transcript of podcast "Jeff Weiner: Leading with Compassion," recorded 9/3/18. https://www.podgist.com/oprahs-supersoul-conversations/jeff-weiner-leading-with-compassion/index.html at marker 8:44-9:41.

Palmer, Parker. *Hidden Wholeness*. San Francisco: Jossey-Bass, 2009.

Penny, Heather. *The Life You're Made For*. Self Published, Heather Penny, 2022.

Solomon, Lou. *Empathy, Chapter 6*. Boston, MA: Harvard Business Review Press, 2017.

Teamwork. "The Importance of Teamwork (as proven by science)," Atlassian, Worklife, posted 1/25/22, https://www.atlassian.com/blog/teamwork/the-importance-of-teamwork.

Thompson, Jeff, PhD. "Is Nonverbal Communication a Number's Game?" Psychology Today. Posted September 30, 2011. https://www.psychologytoday.com/us/blog/beyond-words/201109/is-nonverbal-communication-numbers-game.

Weintraub, Stanley. *Silent Night*. New York City: Plume, 2002.

Zenger, Jack and Joseph Folkman. *HBR Emotional Intelligence series*. Boston, Massachusetts, Harvard Business Review Press, 2017.

Acknowledgments

Words cannot express my gratitude to my editor and friend Natalie Hanemann for her invaluable dedication, guidance, and wisdom. With her gift in listening combined with a clear vision and consistency to excellence, she creates the ideal partnership. It was much of her natural writing ability that helped this book take shape.

I am also grateful to my clients who continue to teach me about what Grace Space gets to mean in the day-to-day living and working environments—to those who continue to put their trust in my coaching and direction. It is their hunger for growth and improvement that continues to inspire me to evolve as a writer, leader, coach, and all-around human.

I cannot leave out my amazing team: Nicole, Cody, Dawn, Amber, and Ryan who continue to cheer me on, believe in my message, listen to all my ideas, join me in creativity, and figure out how to put legs on my vision.

Lastly, I am grateful to my family, who teach me every day what spaces of grace gets to look like. Darren, Selah, and Luke have supported me not only in this writing but in all my projects. They cheer me on by showing up at events just to let me know they care. I always enjoy finding their faces in my audience.

CONNECT WITH ME

heatherpenny.com
facebook.com/HeatherPennyPhD
twitter.com/HeatherPennyPhD
instagram.com/@heatherpennyphd
linkedin.com/in/heather-penny-ph-d-61840414
tiktok.com/@heatherpennyphd

About Dr. Heather Penny

Dr. Heather Penny is a leadership coach and trusted advisor helping individuals and organizations achieve their goals guided by the 3Cs: Clarity, Confidence, and Courage.

With a Ph.D. in Human Services, global coaching experience, and an M.A. in Educational Leadership, she serves leaders and teams to find clarity in their vision, develop confidence in their abilities, and take action.

Dr. Penny's clients range from small businesses to Fortune 500 companies and she has worked with leaders in a variety of industries, including technology, finance, healthcare, and education. Her approach is tailored to the specific needs of each client, and she is known for her ability to quickly get to the heart of the matter and provide practical solutions.

She is a sought-after speaker, host of "The Life You're Made For" podcast, and author of *The Life You're Made For: Finding Clarity, Confidence, and Courage to be Fully Alive*, forwarded by Bob Goff.

Dr. Penny is dedicated to providing the tools and guidance for leaders to identify their strengths and engage in intentional growth.

"[B]uckle up, Heather is about to light a fuse in your life."
—*New York Times* Best-selling Author and Speaker Bob Goff

Want More?
Discover Heather's E-Course at www.heatherpenny.com

Enjoy an excerpt from **The Life You're Made For**:

INTRODUCTION

Finding the Way to Your Dreams

You've been on this journey called life for a while now. So let me ask: Are you closer today to the life you've dreamed of than you were last month?

Okay, maybe the past month was a rough one. And a month is only four weeks. So let me rephrase the question.

Thinking back to where you were a year ago, are you closer today to attaining those dreams than you were then?

Maybe a better question is: Do you even remember what your dreams are? The world has a way of running us hard and wearing us out. Sooner or later, the goal is just to get through the day. There is no thriving. It's just survive today so we can wake up and do it all over again.

But there's more at play. We don't tend to care for ourselves very well. There's no blame here. Most of us were never offered a better way to approach life. We gave it our best shot, but now we're running on empty with little life and downsized dreams.

This way of living isn't sustainable.

If the above paragraphs describe you, I can promise you this. The path you're on won't one day magically lead to where you want to go. Years of traveling in the wrong direction only takes you to a place you never planned to be. And the journey itself will be filled with stress, regret, and a loss of hope. Here's the sobering reality. If you continue in the status quo, doing what you're doing now, life won't even just stay the same. It will likely get worse.

But here's the good news. That isn't the life you were made for. You actually have a choice about which road to take and where it will lead you. You are the driver of your journey, not the victim of circumstances.

The goal of this book is to help you chart a new course toward what makes you come fully alive. It will provide practical ways for you to gain traction in living that better life so you look forward to waking up and living out each day.

I call this process 3C Living.

What are the three "C"s that can change your world? I thought you'd never ask.

> **Clarity.** This is about knowing *who* you are and *where* you want to go.
>
> **Confidence.** This is about what you are believing. If you believe in your potential and the unique strengths you have to offer, it opens up a whole world of new possibility.
>
> **Courage.** This is about taking action and bravely stepping out in new ways. This journey isn't for the timid or halfhearted.

The goal isn't to be partially alive, to settle for a ho-hum-blah existence, or to simply just survive. That isn't the life you were made for.

The goal is to be fully present to the life in front of you and live it out well.

Taken together, 3C Living helps you achieve that. It's not about doing more. You're probably already doing too much—or perhaps you're simply not getting the traction you need to get unstuck. It's about resting more, and then discovering how to do more of what you love while letting go of all that's holding you back! Before we're done, you'll discover how to make the choices you need to supercharge your growing Clarity, Confidence, and Courage.

These proven concepts have transformed my life and the lives of the many students, groups, clients, and companies I have worked with over the years. In fact, you'll hear some of their stories throughout this book.

Remember, you're where you are now because you weren't ready for all the hairpin curves life has put in your path. But you're also closer to breakthrough than you might think. You've just needed a guide (that's me!) to help you get out of that rut and step onto a better path.

Speaking of me, allow me to introduce myself. I'm a teacher, coach, research geek, and regular person who has lived both the "stressed-out life" and the "stuck life," eventually figuring out a better way by using my inborn curiosity and love for personal growth. I geek-out gaining insights on how people grow and develop the same way some love chocolate cake, craft beer, or a deep massage. I know. I'm unique this way. But it's a good uniqueness because I don't just get curious about observations, research, and trends by themselves. My passion is bringing in the human element and applying those findings with ways that lead to us living a better life.

In the early days, I focused my research on the emotional health of high-functioning women as they transitioned from college to the working world. Most studies showed significant signs of depression, anxiety, and fear. Discussions consistently focused on women in this transitional phase as spiraling down. Researchers began identifying this social phenomenon in similar findings across the board.[1] Each research article I read ended with "more research is needed" to address this issue.

I wanted to understand this more so I could help. And logic told me that if people can spiral down, we can also learn to spiral up.

This inspired me to study what made people spiral up rather than down as I focused on two areas: emotional well-being and career fulfillment. Studies frequently focus on the negative point of view, and I was growing tired of reading all the rationale behind what was causing the adverse reactions. I was determined to research how we all—women and men—can live stronger, happier, and more fulfilling lives. I discovered common themes and even created my own terms for what I found. What started out as an initial focus on women actually became applicable to all humanity as I coached people of all ages and genders over the years.

And on a more personal note, my faith is important to me. It centers me and aids me in growing my clarity, confidence, and courage. But it is sacred to me, which I assume it is for you. This is why I don't discuss it throughout this book. I'll leave that for you to integrate as you see fit. But I will reference

---

1. There are many studies that outline this issue. To read more about this, see references listed in endnotes.

it briefly at the end simply to share authentically behind the scenes of what has exponentially worked for me. I do this simply for you to get to know me on a more personal level and to be transparent about what has helped me grow.

So that's me. *I fuse proven research with practical insights for positive change.*

I do this by focusing on what's right—rather than wrong—with people. I take great joy in helping others spiral up, while making the journey enjoyable as they step into their life with renewed purpose. My coaching technique is intentional and purposeful, fueled by love and grace instead of shame or guilt. I focus on you achieving a positive future based on what uniquely fuels *you*. And I want you to know you're never alone on this journey. Over the course of this book, I'll be your guide. But even after that, it's not all up to you. I believe we have people who meet us in our journey exactly when we need them.

So where do we begin? We'll first head to a crossroads where we will pause and catch our breath (doesn't that sound nice?). Then I'll introduce you to some life-changing concepts like Mind Chatter, Tire Swings, Staying Powers, Crossroads, the Belief Snowball, Invisible Pulls, and the Peace of Being.

Our goal isn't to get anywhere fast. It is to get to the right place as a changed human being. Doing so will open our life up to more peace, greater joy, and deeper fulfillment. 3C Living is the map that got me there. It can be your map, too.

I've infused this book with some unique components. For instance, you'll find an allegory—or short story—introducing the book and referenced throughout. Why include it alongside the tangible research, coaching stories, and practical tools? Because I know how powerful stories can be, especially when we are trying to understand new ideas. This simple story allows people to see themselves from a fresh perspective. The story represents the findings of my research in a way that's easy to understand, and it helps me introduce the language I need to talk about complex issues. Using story as a vehicle helps us make the connections necessary to understand the multifaceted issues we are grappling with. I also provide key questions, exercises, and even some helpful "cautions" at the end of every chapter to empower you in staying on track.

This is your invitation to live with new purpose, fresh perspective, and consistent energy. Are you ready to join me on that journey to the life you're made for? If so, turn the page. We'll begin with a story about the things that weigh us down . . . and those that bring us joy.

www.ingramcontent.com/pod-product-compliance
Lightning Source LLC
LaVergne TN
LVHW092050060526
838201LV00047B/1320